cheers to the new
mom!

*tips & tricks to help
you ace the first months
of parenthood*

Jenna McCarthy

SASQUATCH BOOKS
SEATTLE

Printed in Canada
Published by Sasquatch Books
Distributed by PGW/Perseus
15 14 13 12 11 10 09   9 8 7 6 5 4 3 2 1

Cover & interior illustrations: Kate Quinby
Cover & interior design and composition: Kate Basart/Union Pageworks

ISBN-10: 1-57061-558-6
ISBN-13: 978-1-57061-558-0

Sasquatch Books | 119 South Main Street, Suite 400 | Seattle, WA 98104
(206) 467-4300 | www.sasquatchbooks.com | custserv@sasquatchbooks.com

you did it!

You must be feeling pretty proud of yourself right about now. After all, you did it! You made an actual person, practically from scratch. You're someone's **mom**. It really doesn't get much better than that.

Okay, so . . . **now what?**

When you were pregnant, you probably spent countless hours trying to imagine what your new life was going to look like. Friends, family, perfect strangers in Starbucks, and a *teetering pile of books* tried to tell you what to expect, but now you realize that no person and no words could have prepared you for the combination of joy, relief, delirium, awe, and excitement (and possibly a touch of panic and a dash of exhaustion) you would feel the minute you looked into your baby's eyes for the very first time.

Making the decision to **have a child** is **momentous**. It is to **decide forever** to have your *heart* go walking around **outside** your body.

—*Elizabeth Stone*

The only bad news is that most babies don't come with an instruction manual. The really great news is that you don't need one. Most of what you need to know is hardwired in your DNA (they don't call them maternal instincts for nothing). The hardest part will be learning to have faith in those instincts—because surveys show that approximately 100 percent of people you know, love, or accidentally encounter will have an opinion on precisely the best way to *hold, mold, feed, lead, walk, rock, swing, and sing to your baby*. Your friends, your partner, your pediatrician, your own parents, and of course your in-laws will all weigh in, often simultaneously and whether or not you ask them to. When they do, you are encouraged to smile, nod appreciatively, and take it all in—then trust your gut. More often than not, the "right" way to parent is whatever way feels right to *you*. The only absolute: you can't love your baby too much. Everything else is up for discussion.

A mother
is **not** a person
to lean on,
but a person
to make leaning
unnecessary.

—Dorothy Canfield Fisher

Right now you may be thinking: You just warned me about unsolicited new-parent advice! So what's up with this book? Excellent question, even for someone who isn't hormonally challenged and functioning on fifteen minutes of sleep. Here's the thing: this book doesn't care if you listen to it or not. (Your mother-in-law may be another story altogether.) Its feelings won't get hurt if you choose a different approach than one offered on these pages. And it wouldn't dream of gloating when you admit that your impromptu method of swaddling or soothing only served to irritate your already-fussy baby.

If evolution really works, how come mothers only have two hands?

—Milton Berle

Rather than presenting an exhaustive treatise on how to raise your child one particular way, this book offers simple, helpful, low-impact suggestions—yes, *suggestions!*—for making these first months with your baby easier and more enjoyable for everyone involved. And in case you fall so madly in love with that baby—which you will—that you forget that your partner still needs a dose of love and affection—which he does—you will find a few gentle reminders to that effect, too. Also, since you're no good to *anyone* when you're mentally, physically, and emotionally incapacitated, we've included some self-care tips as well—just look for the *Happy Parents Make Happy Babies* icon:

She **never** *quite*
leaves her **children**
at home,

even when
she **doesn't** take

them along.

—*Margaret Culkin Banning*

Will every day with your newborn be rosy-cheeked, Norman Rockwell material? Of course not. Will you make mistakes? Only if you're breathing. Will your child remember any of this? Not a single sleep-deprived minute. Coincidence? Probably not. So relax and enjoy this **magical** time. Ease into it. Get ready to appreciate little things: not only your new little person, but the **small victories**, lessons, and unrepeatable experiences that transform you from a mom-to-be into a mom. It's time to celebrate yourself and your new status as parent. You're going to be great.

Cheers, mom.

Now the thing about
having a baby—
and I can't be
the first person
to have noticed this—
is that thereafter
you have it.

—Jean Kerr

crib
notes

If, despite your near-constant pleas to your partner over the last several months to *assemble the bleeping crib,* you find yourself with a baby at home and nothing remotely resembling a slotted box to put him in, **don't despair**. Like many new parents you might find you want to keep the baby nearby for the first few weeks anyhow, either right in bed with you, in a small, padded co-sleeper that attaches to the side of your bed, or in a bassinet or porta-crib just next to it. This proximity can ease your mind by allowing you to hear every single **wiggle** and **snuffle** from six inches away, while also providing you convenient access to baby for his incessant nighttime feedings. However, if the crib is assembled and ready to go—and you'd prefer he get used to it from the start—you may still want to place a smaller co-sleeper (sometimes called a "snuggle nest") or even a Moses basket inside of it, to create a nice, cozy ambience. (When you lay a tiny newborn in a crib, suddenly it can look cavernous.) And remember, baby monitors today are *state-of-the-art* electronic *eavesdropping* devices—so rest assured you'll still hear every wiggle and snuffle, even from the next room.

SAFETY FIRST!

Always place your baby on his back to sleep, the **safest** position for newborns. When he can roll over from back to front—usually by about **six months**—he gets to choose.

write
on!

The spine creaks as you peel open that beautiful, expensive baby book for the first time. It's so pristine—and you're so tired! What if you mess up? What if your handwriting is utterly illegible? What if the only writing utensil you can find is a dull pencil? Who cares? If you're committed to recording your baby's history, just start writing. It's the effort she'll appreciate, not your flawless penmanship or crack scrapbooking skills. If you haven't gotten around to hunting down the perfect journal yet, or as a supplement to the intimidating baby book, buy an inexpensive calendar or notebook and jot down notes that can be transcribed later. You'll be glad you did.

in case you were
wondering...

* You *will* lose the weight.

* Your baby *won't* cry forever.

* Your sex drive *will* return.

* You *can't* love your baby too much.

* There *isn't* a "right" way to do everything.

* You *will* eventually trust your baby to someone else's care.

* You *will* get the hang of being a mom.

* Visitors *won't* keep popping in unannounced for all of eternity.

* You *will* forget the pain of delivery (many women even decide to do it again!).

The moment a child is born,
the mother is also born.

She never existed before.

The woman existed, but the
mother, never.

**A mother is something
absolutely new.**

—*Rajneesh*

1 5

HAPPY PARENTS *make* HAPPY BABIES

Let it go

Adjusting to new-mom speed can be tough, especially for superachievers. When mounting piles of laundry, dirty dishes, unopened mail, and unmade beds are making you crazy, remind yourself that this is a temporary phase in your life. Then focus on what is really important: getting rest and loving your baby and your partner. Will it matter in five weeks—or five months or five years—that you sent the thank-you notes a little late? That you cooked frozen pizza three nights in a row? That you had dust bunnies waltzing in the corner of your living room? It's time to alter your expectations of what you thought could get done in a day, and let go. Your baby will only be a newborn for a very short time. Enjoy it. The laundry can wait.

sound
advice

Creeping around and shushing people every time the baby is sleeping seems like simple good manners—not to mention potentially conducive to long stretches of slumber (at least for the baby). Create an unnaturally still environment, though, and you run the risk of cultivating a child that wakes at the slightest **whisper** or **wind shift**. Newborns are natural sleepers; in fact, sometimes it's harder to keep them awake than to get them to sleep. Get her used to napping through your usual household background noise now—chatting, flushing toilets, even vacuuming—and it'll never seem intrusive to her.

fun
parenting facts!*

4.3   Number of babies born each second

25   Average age of first-time moms in the U.S. (up from 21 in 1970)

2 minutes, 5 seconds   Average time it takes a mom to diaper a baby

69   Record number of children birthed by a single woman

330   Loads of laundry done by average mom in a year

7,300   Number of diaper changes baby will undergo by second birthday (note: this number, multiplied by the 2 minutes 5 seconds per change, totals six and a half 40-hour work weeks of diaper changing)

Source: happyworker.com

People who say
they sleep
like babies
usually don't
have them.

—Leo J. Burke

upgrade your memory

When the congratulations cards start pouring in, use a pretty box or gift bag (like one left over from your shower) to store them in. Not only will they be fun to look at later, but if a card comes with a gift, you can jot a quick note on the back, toss it in the box, and know where to find it. This information will be extremely valuable in the likely event it takes you a while to get to your thank-you cards. (Later, you can add in all those special first-birthday cards—which will arrive before you know it!—and you'll have an amazing family keepsake.)

company
policy

You will never again in your life be as popular as you are when you first bring home a new baby. Friends, relatives, neighbors, and co-workers will beg to drop by, often with hot and hearty meals in hand. *Do not feel bad about this for a second*—in fact, encourage it! Under no circumstance should you *ever* say, "Oh, there's no need to bring anything." Even if your fridge and freezer are fully stocked, when your visitors ask what you need, it's okay (really) to have them pick up toilet paper, Tylenol, a package of diapers, a carton of ice cream, or anything else you're running low on to save you a trip. People (especially those who have been there) really do want to help—be gracious and let them.

Every beetle is a gazelle in the *eyes* of its **mother**.

—*Moorish proverb*

holy hormones!

One moment you're on top of the world—intoxicated by the sweet smell of your powder-fresh baby— the next you feel completely OVERWHELMED. You laugh, cry, swear, and sweat enough for a full Broadway ensemble— and that was just in the last five minutes. And you thought PMS was bad! The mood swings you're experiencing are frustrating, yet they're entirely normal. Alas, the things that will tip the hormonal scales in your favor again (sunlight, sleep, exercise, sleep, healthy food, sleep) are the hardest to come by right now. Try to get as much of the good stuff as you can, and in the meantime, know that it's okay to cry or vent as needed for release. Do try to remember that this "new normal" is only temporary; it will not last for the duration of motherhood. You'll be yourself again before you know it.

carry on

There's nothing more comforting to a baby than the sound of your voice and the **warmth** of your body. *Of course* she is going to protest when these things are taken away from her. Still, you've got stuff to do that can't be done when you're cradling an infant all day. Invest in a sling or front carrier, and everyone wins. Strap her in and then tackle some light household chores, go for a **stroll**, bake something sinful, pick up some takeout, or take her on her first shopping excursion. (Since you probably won't feel like trying on clothes for a while, she won't be in the way at all.)

There **never**
was a child
so lovely
but his **mother**
was glad
to get him
asleep.

—Ralph Waldo Emerson

beware the
peanut gallery

It probably happened the split second you announced your pregnancy—maybe even when you admitted you were "trying": helpful folks *crawled out of the woodwork* to offer their suggestions on just about every aspect of pregnancy and parenthood. "You *have* to get this prenatal vitamin/HypnoBirthing CD/maternity underwear/nursing pillow," they insist, and you're left speechless and feeling utterly idiotic. *Does motherhood really render women unable to pick out their own underpants?* you wonder. Sure, sometimes the advice is actually helpful, but it can also be **overwhelming**. Sadly, the unwelcome assistance doesn't stop when the baby is born.

Being prepared with an assortment of well-rehearsed and *socially appropriate comebacks* can prevent you from unleashing any pent-up hostility on your self-appointed savior. When the advice arrives in the form of a statement ("So-and-so makes the best baby blankets *ever!*"), a simple "Thanks for the tip!" is often sufficient. However, when you're barraged with questions ("Are you going to breastfeed/go back to work/sleep with the baby?"), there's almost always a "correct" answer implied. You could throw out a casual "We haven't decided on that yet," although this isn't likely to put an end to the discussion. The ever-popular "My doctor recommended *xyz*" can get you out of a lot of sticky spots; you also might consider turning the tables: "I'm not sure; I know that there are arguments for both sides. What did *you* do?" This gives the adviser an opportunity to tell you how **brilliant** she is, which is really all she wants anyhow. Follow whatever she says with "Good to know!" (even if it's not), and leave it at that.

ways your life has changed that you didn't expect

1. You mark the passage of time in weeks.

2. When someone calls out "mom" in a restaurant, mall, or other crowded place, you automatically turn your head.

3. You suddenly see babies everywhere, and you are compelled to ask their ages and their names, then tell the parents how beautiful their offspring are (even though you secretly believe that yours is cuter).

4. You realize just how little sleep you need to function.

5. No matter what your relationship was or is, you have developed a new level of respect for your own parents.

6. You become masterful at performing silly, forgetful acts—and later, genuinely cannot explain how your razor got into the freezer.

7. You have grown to admire and respect your body in a way that has nothing to do with thin thighs or toned arms.

8. You will find ways to use the words "my son" or "my daughter" dozens of times a day.

9. It occurs to you that your dog—whom you love beyond measure—is just a dog.

10. You fall in love with your partner all over again.

A **mother** is a **person** who **seeing** there are only **four** pieces of pie for *five* people, promptly announces she **never did** care for pie.

—Tenneva Jordan

cutting
the cord

You might be hard-pressed to find a new mom who enjoys looking at the shriveled, drying-out *thing* attached to her otherwise unblemished baby's middle (especially when you consider that the other end of that *thing* used to be attached to you, a reality that just doesn't seem possible). Rest assured that within three weeks, the umbilical stump—that's really what it's called—will be but a distant memory. In the meantime, clean the area around it gently with warm water only (alcohol was yesterday's news; pediatricians now advise against using it), and be careful to fold her diapers down and away so as not to irritate it. Wait to administer her first real bath until the stump (sorry) has fallen off naturally.

spit
happens

Spit-up is a fact of newborn life. These episodes can range from tiny wet **hiccups** to a powerful projectile spray. The most common cause is an excess of air swallowed along with milk or formula. Obviously, the first line of defense is always having a stash of soft **burp cloths** nearby, especially during feedings (buy them in bulk!). Other helpful tips:

* **Don't let baby get too hungry.** The faster he eats, the more air he's likely to swallow. And what goes down too quickly often comes back up.

* **Use the natural pauses** he takes during feeding as opportunities to burp. The more frequently you do this, the less liquid is likely to be expelled.

* **Keep him upright** for a half hour after eating, and allow gravity to help keep his food down.

* **If he acts like he's had enough**, trust him on it. Remember, his tummy is tiny, and overfeeding generally leads to overflowing.

basket
case

It's feeding time, and you plop down on the couch and prepare to offer your babe either breast or bottle. You're nicely situated and immediately the phone starts to ring. You retrieve it and sit back down, readjust, and realize you're desperately thirsty. Once again, you pop up, get yourself a drink, and return to the couch. From here you spot the pile of magazines on the far table, the ones you've been itching to peruse. Ah, if only they were within arm's reach . . .

Savvy moms keep a portable "feeding necessities" kit at the ready at all times. Get yourself a pretty little tote or basket (handles are key), and throw in some burp cloths, a water bottle, reading material, a sweater or wrap, and some socks for you *and* baby, plus a baggie or small Tupperware container of nonperishable snacks like nuts, trail mix, or pretzels. When feeding time rolls around, toss your cordless or cell phone on top and you'll be good to go (or rather, stay).

dreaming of sleep?

If you're lucky, your baby is a natural-born sleeper. If you're not, your choices are basically wait it out, cry it out, or constantly go back and forth. These suggestions might help you to get through-the-night more quickly.

* **Establish a bedtime ritual**. One that works for lots of folks is also easy to remember: bath, book, breast or bottle, bed. He'll soon learn where this sequence of events is leading and may start yawning as soon as he hears the tub filling up.

* **Resist the urge** to *always* bounce/rock/hold him until he's fast asleep. You want him to learn the skill of self-soothing, and that can only be accomplished if he's allowed to fall asleep on his own. Try putting him down when he's drowsy but not completely out.

* **Help him learn** to differentiate between (short) day and (long) night sleep. There comes a point when babies are waking every two hours all night long not because they're hungry, but because they just enjoy your company so darned much. Try being "all business" during the night by simply feeding, changing, and returning him to his crib with no lights, chatter, songs, or otherwise engaging activities.

the joy
of sacks

If you don't know what a sleep sack is yet, you're missing the midnight boat. These wonder garments look like elongated dresses, come in cozy cotton or microfleece, and will quickly become your new nighttime best friends. Some are elasticized but open at the bottom (like a long gown); others have a single, easy-to-find zipper that goes from bottom to top. When it's time for a diaper change, there are no snaps or ties to **fiddle** with; simply find your baby's feet, hike up the sack, and you're half-way home. The thicker varieties of sleep sacks also serve as wearable blankets, so you don't have to worry about junior catching a chill when he invariably kicks out of his swaddling blanket. Plus, the fact that they are tangle-proof puts them at the top of the safe list. In a word: **genius**.

be a
groupie

Even if you're not a joiner by nature, finding other new parents to bond with can be an invaluable experience. You'll enjoy adult conversation, **camaraderie**, and commiseration now, and shared babysitting and playdates later. These **benefits** cannot be overstated. Check with your pediatrician, OB office, or birthing hospital for established new-parent programs you can join, or start your own with co-workers, neighbors, and friends.

turn the
tables

A fussy baby often is a bored baby, and at no time will this be more obvious than when he is on his changing table. Consider using the airspace above him as a rotating art installation. Try some—or all—of the following ideas to keep him entertained (read: distracted) long enough to get the deed done. You might even find you have five minutes to relax while he checks out the scene!

* **A small mobile** (no need to spend a mint; a simple model can be handcrafted from a hanger and a few colorful pieces of ribbon)

* **Colorful swatches** of fabric or patterned wallpaper taped to the wall ("What do you think about this combo for the guest bathroom?")

* **A wind chime** (audio *and* visual stimulation—score!)

* **Black-and-white** geometric patterns (with a Sharpie and a piece of scrap paper, your kid won't know you're not Picasso)

* **A family photo** ("See how young and rested mommy used to look?")

* **A ceiling fan** (pricey, sure, but in the long run could cut down on your air-conditioning bill *and* save your sanity)

* **A small, unbreakable mirror** like the ones made for car seats (babies are as narcissistic as the rest of us; his own face is sure to captivate)

Pop psychology

Yes, it's fair to say that you have done most of the work up until this point: you conceived, carried, and birthed a human being, for heaven's sake! Still, imagine how left-out your partner may have been feeling, and will probably continue to feel, especially if you are nursing the baby constantly and he can't really share that load. Take a moment to stop what you are doing, and tell him that you love and appreciate him. Tell him he's going to make a great dad. (He worries, too.) Tell him all the specific little things he's doing beautifully so far. Verbally acknowledging this is good for both of you (and may make him quicker to forgive you when you snap at him ten minutes from now).

HAPPY PARENTS
make
HAPPY BABIES

Biology
is the **least**
of what **makes**
someone
a **mother**.

—*Oprah Winfrey*

a star
is born

Announcing your baby's birth is one of the great joys of new parenthood. But you've been so busy and tired, and now it's been two months—or eight. Did you miss the window? Unless she's busy filling out college applications, it's rarely too late to announce baby's arrival. Photo Web sites like Shutterfly and Kodakgallery make it super easy—just download her photo, add her vitals (name, birth date, weight/length), and submit your order. Once your package arrives, give yourself some sort of timeline—say, address three cards a day or ten a week—and definitely enlist the help of your partner or a friend. Just be warned: sending out announcements often results in a cascade of gifts—lovely to be sure, but they do require thank-you notes as well. (While you're online, perhaps ordering a few dozen of these—and some cute stamps from the post office—will put you ahead in the game.)

We spend the **first** *twelve* months of our **children's** lives *teaching* them to **walk** and **talk** and the next **twelve** telling them to **sit down** and shut up.

—*Phyllis Diller*

for crying out loud!

Your baby is fussy and you're at the breaking point. Don't give up hope—try one or more of these soothing tricks. One of them is bound to work:

✳ **Whisper sweet nothings**. Hold her close to your body and gently sway back and forth as you murmur "shhhhhh, shhhhhh, shhhhhh" into her ear at a pretty good volume. This goes beyond the power of suggestion; that whooshing sound actually mimics the womb ambience she grew to know and love. Many babies will quiet immediately upon hearing this refrain.

✳ **Might as well jump**. Again, remember that to date, the only environment she knows intimately is the inside of your body. Rarely was she static in there. Motion is familiar and therefore comforting to her. Sit on the edge of a bed, or purchase a large exercise ball or minitrampoline, and get in a little workout while you're at it. (When she gets bigger she'll love playing with either of these, so they're sound long-term investments.)

✳ **Pacify her**. Literally. Suckling is naturally soothing to babies (and while you might think you don't want to go down the synthetic-sucker road, know that she'll eventually find her thumb or fingers, which are much harder to take away when you're ready to wean her). Pacifiers come in dozens of shapes and sizes for a reason: all babies prefer different models, typically the one you buy last. Having an assortment on hand is helpful. Newborns also enjoy sucking on their parents' clean pinkie fingers—something dad can help with, too.

* **Consider the ambience**. Since you likely can't—or won't want to—hold and "shhhhhh" her 24/7, smart companies have designed an army of CDs, noise machines, and plush toys that feature all manner of relaxing sounds and melodies. From traditional lullabies to chirping crickets, from windshield wipers to human heartbeats, there's a sound out there to calm and comfort just about every babe on the block.

* **Pump up the volume**. It may sound counterintuitive, but parents often report their babies find loud music, annoying radio static, or even a rowdy sporting match on TV more soothing than a whispered lullaby. Again, all babies are different, and you won't know what floats her boat until you try it.

* **Be a good mummy**. In other words, learn how to swaddle. This little trick is probably the most underrated weapon in the parenting arsenal. You see, babies are born with a startle reflex (technically called the "Moro reflex") that inconveniently seems to rear its ugly head precisely as they start to drift off to sleep. If they didn't show you how to swaddle in the hospital, Google it, buy a book on it, pick up a designated "swaddle blanket" that comes with instructions, or ask a veteran mom friend to show you the ropes. You'll probably do it until she is at least four or five months old, so it's worth learning to swaddle well.

stop
watching
the *clock*

As anxious as you are for your baby to sit/crawl/walk, know that the more mobile she is, the less freedom *you* have. Hurry up and indulge in her immobility while you still can. Plop her onto her play mat, swing, or vibrating infant seat with some engaging toys, and hop into the bathtub. Shave your legs *and* condition your hair while you're in there. She's still content? Scrub your feet, knees, and elbows with a soft pumice stone. You're not ignoring her; you're **fostering** her **independence**. Just don't fall asleep in there, okay?

Motherhood is,
after all,
woman's
great and
incomparable
work.

—Edward Carpenter

be
prepared

No matter how painstakingly you pack your diaper bag, the day will come when you reach in there and discover the last diaper is the dirty one you just tossed into the trash. Be a savvy mom and keep a backup stash of necessities in the car and another set in the stroller. A ziploc bag with two diapers and a few wipes will save you again and again—just don't forget to replace the ones you use.

The hand that rocks the cradle usually is attached to someone who *isn't* getting enough sleep.

—John Fiebig

other disaster-prevention tips for new moms

* **Have an emergency contact** list pasted to your phone and also at a central location in your house (on the fridge or a bulletin board). It should include your home address, phone number, pediatrician's name, closest hospital and clinic, and insurance information, as well as the phone numbers of two or three nearby friends to call in an emergency.

* **Create a file** in your home to store important data about your baby (medical records, social security information, cord blood banking info, etc.). Without this, you might think that you'll remember that you temporarily put her passport in the pet folder, but you probably won't.

* **Assemble a stash** of extra essentials for each vehicle you use. Stock a box or bag with extra diapers, formula, a bottle, bibs, toys, water, pacifiers, a sun hat, small travel blanket, a towel, and spare clothes. (Throw in a change for yourself for those occasions when she throws up on the both of you, and score extra points!)

* **Find some cute** luggage tags and load them with vital information: baby's name and birthday, parents' names and contact information, pediatrician's phone and address, and important allergy or medical info, if applicable. Attach one each to the stroller, car seat, and primary diaper bag.

* **Ziploc bags!** The importance of these treasures cannot be overstated until you carry around a stinky diaper for an hour looking for a trash bin. Keep a stockpile on hand at all times.

* **Buy batteries in bulk:** You'll go through them like Kleenex. Virtually every toy, vibrating seat, musical swing, monitor, and mobile you own will demand them, and they need replacing constantly— especially in the middle of the night. Now that you have your very own future generation to protect, consider investing in rechargeable batteries. They're better for the environment and also will save you a wad of cash in the long run.

* **Optional but awesome:** Pick up a few disposable cameras and stick one in your stroller, glove box, and diaper bag. Often you'll find yourself in situations where your baby looks adorable, the lighting is spectacular, and the camera is tucked away safely at home.

All soles go to heaven

Pedicures probably dropped off your priority list when you could no longer see your toes. Now that they're back in your line of sight, give 'em some love! This isn't just about cracked heels or chipped polish. You need pampering, big-time. Fortunately, your little peanut is wonderfully portable right now, so if you can't get someone to watch him for an hour, bring him along! Park him beside you in his car seat or stroller, then sit back and relax while your limbs are lavished with TLC and your baby is ogled appreciatively by hordes of strangers.

HAPPY PARENTS
make
HAPPY BABIES

security measures

Remember Charlie Brown's lovable little friend Linus, the guy who dragged his scraggly blue blanket everywhere? Well, it turns out the munchkin was onto something. In doc-talk, security blankets are called "transitional objects," and most babies will naturally glom on to one to make separating from you easier. The object of a baby's affection is likely to be something familiar to her, so right now you have the power to sway this life-altering decision. Find a small, soft stuffed animal *that is machine washable* (you cannot imagine the abuse this item will take) or mini blanket square and place it in her crib or bassinet from day one. Leaving the selection of the transitional object to your baby increases the risk that she will become attached to, say, one of your couch cushions or the dog's bed, which would be disastrous in terms of practicality and portability. Consider buying *two identical* items, to avoid a meltdown in the inevitable case one gets misplaced or puked on. If you're still pregnant, you might even want to start sleeping with your chosen item(s) *now* so that your deliciously comforting scent is transferred to it/them. Worth considering: the darker the object, the better it will wear over the long haul. (Remember, this trinket may accompany you on every airplane ride, car trip, pediatrician appointment, and countless other outings for the next five years or more.)

seven fun things to do with your baby

1. **Take a million photos** of him and e-mail them to everyone in your address book. Everyone appreciates an adorable baby—and a chance to take a break from boring work. When he starts doing cute tricks—smiling, waving, rolling over—upgrade to quick video clips.

2. **Have a contest** to see which of your friends can nail the celebrity your new babe most resembles. (Note: babies frequently resemble bald males such as Dennis Franz, Bruce Willis, Samuel L. Jackson, and yes, occasionally Homer Simpson.)

3. **Splurge on a pretty baby book** and catalog his every yawn. Even if you think you'll remember each important milestone, in your sleep-deprived state some are sure to slip through the cracks.

4. **Make up silly songs** featuring his name—and get creative! You may be surprised to find how many words rhyme with Olivia or Oscar when you employ poetic license. When you stumble across some great lyrics, record them in his baby book.

5. **Get out of the house.** Sometimes all it takes to soothe a bored or fussy baby is a change of scenery (and most parents report that outdoor scenes work

best). If weather permits, take a stroll through a nearby park or outdoor shopping center. Weather not on your side? Bundle up, sit in a cozy coffee shop together, and bask in the beautiful-baby comments.

6. **Buy an inexpensive tape recorder** (yes, they still make them; you can find them at most office-supply stores) and capture his dazzling repertoire of sounds. It's lighter and cheaper than your video camera, so you won't be afraid to tote it all over town; just stash it in your diaper bag and you'll never miss an adorable peep. (Some parents have found that hearing his own sounds can be very soothing—or at least intriguing—to a baby.)

7. **Take a nap together**. There is nothing in the world more intoxicating than the smell and feel of a tiny baby nuzzled next to you. Sweet dreams!

drop
your drawers

Once your baby is sitting up, one of his favorite activities will be opening and closing every drawer within reach. If your setup is flexible, make some of the lower ones as kid-friendly and intriguing as possible. Move your Tupperware and some wooden utensils to a bin he can access—he'll spend hours removing, stacking, sorting, and, yes, tossing and banging them around. In your bedroom, maybe some of his books or soft toys could be relocated to your bottom dresser or nightstand drawer. Always watch him closely as he's playing with drawers; when little fingers get pinched, big wails often follow.

A baby will make
love stronger,
days **shorter**,
nights longer,
bankroll smaller,
home happier,
clothes **shabbier**,
the past forgotten,
and the **future**
worth living for.

—*Unknown*

host (hōst); n.

1. One who *entertains* guests in a **social capacity**.

2. An *organism* on which a **parasite** lives.

For many new parents, the baby's homecoming coincides with back-to-back (sometimes unwanted) houseguests. Your parents, his parents, a sister, aunt, or family friend may well just show up on your doorstep—along with a stack of steamer trunks—and offer to "help." Even if this person is only *slightly less welcome than a Rottweiler*, invite her in **warmly**. Remember, he or she (but most likely she) is there to help *you*, and the best way to make sure that happens is by establishing the rules right out of the gate. **Do not clean** for her, attempt to **entertain** her, or **wait on** her in any capacity. (She's *not* a guest, she's a temporary servant.) Show her where things are and tell her specifically how she can be most helpful. Give her a list of specific tasks (wash/fold this pile of laundry, boil the bottles in that cabinet, pick up these particular diapers), and be sure to specify the things you *don't* want her to do ("We know you have a great eye for design, but we really like our furniture arranged this way, thanks!"). Most important: make sure she knows in advance how long the welcome mat will be out. Even if you love and enjoy her company and she's utterly helpful and not at all obtrusive, you will eventually yearn for some time alone with your new family.

HAPPY PARENTS *make* HAPPY BABIES

Sleep on it

Remember that guy you're married to? You know, the one who helped you make the baby? As hard as it is to be patient and loving toward him when you need toothpicks to prop open your eyelids, you're in this together for the long haul. Believe it or not, the one thing your marriage probably needs the most isn't therapy or even a date night (although those things probably wouldn't hurt), it's *sleep*. If baby's quiet, grab your guy and snuggle up for a nap together. Get it wherever and whenever you can, and do it without an ounce of guilt. Step up and lie down!

he's
melting!

If it hasn't happened yet, it will: his first major public meltdown. This won't be fun for either of you, not only because of the ghastly looks you will receive from judgmental onlookers, but also because you will feel helpless and pathetic. All you can do is try to figure out the source of his distress (Is he hungry? Wet? Tired? Bored? Overstimulated?) and remedy it as quickly as possible. Sometimes, it's best just to scrap the immediate plans and change the scene. Remember that this happens to *all* mothers from time to time, and it is not a sign of inadequacy. Your baby has very few jobs right now, and one of his primary ones is to cry. It won't kill him (even if it feels like it's killing you) and hopefully, no one is videotaping the incident for posterity. And think of it this way: the more it happens, the more you'll be prepared for when he turns two.

look mom, no hands!

For the next several months—possibly years—you will not have two simultaneously free hands. Investing in a quality headset for both your home and cell phones will enable you to enjoy the occasional chat with a friend. Now, no one is suggesting you wear or use the thing constantly, but when baby is asleep on stroller rides, or you're trapped under her sleeping body on the couch, or she's snoozing in the car—finally—while you do laps around the block, you'll be glad you have this little luxury on hand.

exercise your
options

You may not realize this yet, but your baby makes a great workout partner. Mom-and-baby fitness classes allow you to keep him close by in an atmosphere that doesn't just tolerate feeding/changing/soothing stops but actively encourages them. **Bonus:** no childcare fees and no heartbreaking parting moments. Another, less strenuous option: colleges, community centers, libraries, and even some bookstores offer mom/baby story time, play time, and more. Look on a local mom message board, in the paper, or online for activities you can do as a duo.

simple sleep
test

You rocked/swayed/bounced her to sleep—at least you *think* she's asleep. Now what? Should you put her down? Will she wake up? Try this nifty trick: gently lift one of her little hands an inch or two from your body and release it. If she resists or tries to grasp your finger, she's not quite to la-la land yet. On the other hand, if her hand drops with no resistance whatsoever, it's probably safe to attempt to lay her down. Do it as slowly and gently as possible, preferably into a Moses basket or co-sleeper that will feel almost as cozy as your body.

Take a backseat

Remember, you can encourage your partner to spend time with the baby—but you can't tell him what to do or how to do it. He'll hold, rock, feed, dress, and swaddle differently than you do—and that's okay. In fact, you might learn some new tricks from him! There's more than one way to juice a lemon, as they say. Instead of hovering over the two of them and biting your tongue, whenever possible use their bonding time to put your feet up or get out of the house solo. (And do praise him for a job well done when you return.)

a room of one's own

When you're ready to transition your baby from your bed or the bassinet into her own crib, a few simple tricks can make the move a lot easier:

* If she's been *snoozing in your room*, you might consider placing her crib in there, too, until she gets used to it. (Then when you move the entire crib to her room, she's a lot less likely to protest because it's already a familiar space—sort of.)

* Introduce her to her crib during the day—not at night, when she expects you to be within arm's reach. Spend some time *tickling her belly*, smiling at her, or playing peekaboo in there, establishing it as a happy place.

* Many a babe has been enthralled by the sight of a *strategically placed mobile* over the crib—and many a mom has snuck from the nursery unnoticed as a result. (If she's a big fan of the one over the changing table, use that one or a duplicate for familiarity.)

* Place your own unwashed pillowcase, nightgown, or yes, even a nursing pad or bra in her crib. (If she's mobile, tie it to the crib bars rather than placing anything in the crib itself.) Babies have *powerful little noses*, and this might trick her into thinking that you're closer than you actually are.

armed
to the teeth

Believe it or not, the time to start caring for his tiny little teeth is actually before they even burst through his gums. The sooner you get your baby used to the insult of having any sort of tool jammed into his mouth, the less likely he is to resist it. In fact, start while he's **teething** and he'll probably be eager to gum his new toothbrush for hours (no toothpaste just yet). The American Academy of Pediatric Dentistry suggests scheduling his first dental visit right around his first birthday—at that point you can inquire about professional cleanings, whether or when you should introduce **toothpaste**, and if fluoride supplementation is necessary in your area.

chew *on* this

When your little love starts eating solid food at around six months, you may feel like you spend half your day in the kitchen. These tips will help get you in and out of there in a jiffy:

* **Weather permitting**, strip her down to a diaper before a feeding. It's easier to wipe her down than wash five outfits a day (and even with a bib, she's likely to wind up wearing at least some of her meal).

* **Have her food ready**—pureed/chopped/in the bowl—before you put her in her high chair. If she has to sit there and wait for you to prep her plate, she may become too agitated to eat.

* **When feeding her with a spoon**, have another spoon on hand for her to hold and play with. This may diminish her insistence on trying to get yours away from you.

* **If you're making homemade** baby food, whip up a big batch and spoon it into a clean ice cube or mini-muffin tray, then pop it into the freezer. You'll have at least a dozen premade, home-cooked meals at the touch of a button.

* **When she graduates** to self-feeding, the stickier the consistency, the more food will adhere to her fork, spoon, or fingers. Fewer trips from bowl to mouth translate into a quicker, easier meal.

While we **try** to teach
our **children** all about life,
our children teach us
what **life is** all about.

—*Unknown*

RECYCLING
TIP!

Now that you're buying bananas in bulk, lots of them are likely to turn brown on your countertop. When they are ripe beyond the point of edibility, peel and wrap each one individually in tinfoil, then stick them in the freezer. When they're good and frozen, toss one in the blender with some milk or yogurt, juice, and any fruit you have handy for a delicious, nutritious smoothie. (The bananas give it a rich, creamy consistency without watering down the texture like ice would.)

Note: if you're sharing your smoothie with your baby, be sure every ingredient is on the approved list.

signs you've survived early parenthood

1. You can turn the baby monitor off for five or even ten minutes at a stretch.

2. Sometimes you leave the house with a bag smaller than your microwave oven.

3. You have no idea what they're hawking on those midnight infomercials anymore.

4. When you go to the hospital to meet your best friend's newborn, your own baby looks like a moose in comparison.

5. You find yourself offering unsolicited advice to perfect strangers with small babies.

6. You occasionally initiate sex.

7. At any given moment you can extract a crayon, goldfish cracker, or pacifier from the depths of your bag without even looking.

8. You no longer have to consult a checklist before heading out of the house.

9. Clothes shopping sounds appealing again.

10. You start toying with the idea of having . . . another baby.

signs you've survived early parenthood

1. Your wife is speaking to you.

2. The bags under your eyes are no longer visible from the next zip code.

3. You can manage formerly challenging tasks (changing a diaper, cubing grapes, and hooking your baby safely into his car seat) with one hand.

4. You casually tell your wife you're hungry—in baby sign language.

5. You finally have more beer than breast milk in your refrigerator.

6. You've seen at least one of the (nonanimated) films up for the Best Picture Oscar.

7. You can fit back into the jeans you wore on your honeymoon.

8. You no longer cringe every time the doorbell or phone rings.

9. You've quit swearing (but if you absolutely have to let a profanity fly, you automatically spell the offensive words).

10. You don't actually need to read the words to any of your child's books because you know them all by heart.

The father who does not teach his son his duties is equally guilty with the son who neglects them.

—Confucius

Having a child is *surely* the most **beautifully** irrational act that two people **in love can commit**.

—*Bill Cosby*

The **child** had
every toy his
father wanted.

—*Robert C. Whitten*

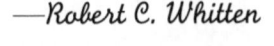

into the mouths of babes

Babies love putting things in their mouths—it's one of human nature's most instinctive means of exploration. When she's in this phase, watch her like a hawk and use this as a general rule of thumb: if an **object** is **small** enough to slide through a toilet paper or paper towel tube, it could be a choking hazard. Start putting all your loose change in a jar out of reach, learn to scan the vicinity regularly for everything from buttons to gravel to nutshells, and take any small objects she finds away immediately.

looks from your fellow travelers if your child screams for the duration of the trip.

* **Buy him his own seat**, especially if you can use frequent-flier miles to do so. It's the safest place for him, gives you a bit more space, and offers some flexibility in terms of which of the passengers in front of you you'd like to annoy the most with his incessant kicking/screaming/food tossing.

* **Change your baby's diaper** at the very last possible moment before boarding. If you think those airplane lavatories are small when you're solo, just wait until you try to clean and freshen a baby in there.

* **Don't spring for the** headphones. When was the last time you got to watch a two-hour movie? It's not going to happen, and knowing that in advance will make you much less resentful.

* **Pack distractions**. A few extra-special, never-before-seen books, toys, and snacks will work wonders.

flying by the seat of your pants

There may come a time in the not-distant future when you decide to take your baby to a far-away place. Sometimes the only way to reach such a place is by airplane. Should such a situation arise, just about all you can do is memorize the tips here and cross your fingers:

* **When you hear** the announcement that "Passengers traveling with small children may board now," you may want to ignore it (unless your baby is sound asleep in an infant car seat). Sure, it's easier to struggle up that nine-inch-wide aisle with your copious belongings when there aren't large bodies filling the seats; however, the last thing you need right now is an extra forty-five minutes of sardine-sitting tacked on to your trip.

* **Reconfigure your priorities.** You used to always fly the red-eye, direct. (You also used to play poker every Sunday night, train for triathlons, and read the paper on a daily basis. Get over it.) Layovers aren't so bad with babies; in fact, the change of scenery often does you both a world of good. As far as the red-eye goes, a baby may or may not sleep on a plane, regardless of the time of day or night you schedule your flight. At least during daytime flights you'll get significantly fewer nasty

A *baby* is **born** with the need **to be** **loved**—and **never** outgrows it.

—Frank A. Clark

clothes
call

While your partner might be guilty of wrapping the baby in one too many layers of subzero protection, there's a remote chance you might err on the other end of the temperature spectrum. When you take him outside, remember you're the one pushing the stroller/hiking uphill/pedaling the bike. He's just along for the (possibly nippy) ride. While he might not need a full-body down snowsuit on a spring morning, the general rule is to dress baby in one layer more than you or your partner would enjoy for the given activity. And don't forget his head.

HAPPY PARENTS make HAPPY BABIES

The lost boys

Feel like you never see your buddies anymore? When you have a baby, friends without kids might find it hard to relate (and no offense, but you probably talk about the kid *a lot*). This is simply an adjustment phase and usually works itself out. In the meantime, use some of your lonely downtime to reconnect with those pals *you* blew off when they had kids and you didn't. They'll more than likely be eager to welcome you back into the fold. The smoothest way to get together with other dads or single friends is to have them over to your place, or go out for a beer after baby's bedtime when your work at home is done. (Chances are your wife will be sound asleep by then, too, and won't mind at all.)

hammer
time

The more mobile your baby becomes, the more you may grow convinced that danger lurks behind every door and drawer in the house. While there is no substitute for your vigilance, storing poisonous chemicals out of reach and locking up sharp or dangerous items is just smart parenting. And childproofing the house, which requires both tools and patience, often falls to dad, so hit a home run here for your family's peace of mind. Get online or go to your local Target or hardware store and stock up on those plastic doorknob covers, drawer and cabinet locks, and a mother lode of outlet covers—since roughly every child under the age of five will attempt at least once to jam something into an electrical outlet to see what happens. (Commando tip: when you run out of covers or you're on the road, duct tape may not look too chic, but it does the job.) While you're at it, move all medicines, cleaners, and other truly toxic items up to the highest shelf the adults can reach for added security.

When I was a boy of fourteen, my father was so ignorant I could hardly stand to have the old man around. But when I got to be twenty-one, I was astonished at how much he had learned in seven years.

—Mark Twain

extra! extra!

Read all about it: a dad takes his new-born baby on an outing. When the time comes to return home, the wily guy opens the back door of his SUV, tosses his keys into the driver's seat—where he will be able to conveniently retrieve them in just a moment—and goes about the business of strapping his infant safely into the car. Mission accomplished, he gently but firmly slams the rear door . . . only to realize to his great horror that all of the doors are locked. And his keys are inside the car. *With the baby.* Don't be this guy. Have spare keys made for every car you drive, and make sure your partner has one, your neighbor has one, the junk drawer in your office has one, and that there's a hide-a-key somewhere on the actual car. You might as well make sure you have a spare house key hidden somewhere while you're at it. Hopefully you'll never need to use any of them, but why take the chance?

Having a baby changes the way you view your in-laws. I love it when *they* come to visit now. They can hold the baby and I can go out.

—*Matthew Broderick*

sound
off

It's no secret that babies love music. Who cares if your wife's rendition of "Rock-a-Bye Baby" blows yours out of the water? You're the air guitar champ! And your audience is pretty easy to please. If the only lyrics you know belong to the fight song from your alma mater, sing it loud and proud, dad. Or bust out your best AC/DC, Red Hot Chili Peppers, 50 Cent, or Louis Armstrong. Don't expect a standing ovation—but you might stumble upon a definite crowd-pleaser that's fun and entertaining for both of you.

The same rule applies to books. Your baby is interested in the sound of your voice, not the surprise ending to "Goldilocks and the Three Bears." Nevertheless, reading to her from an early age is important if you want to instill in her a love of learning and books. So hunker down on the couch with her and peruse the *Wall Street Journal*, *Sports Illustrated*, the Sharper Image catalog, or Dave Barry's latest riff on politics or suburban life. Score bonus points for incorporating funny accents and amusing sound effects.

"I don't know **why** *they say* 'you have a baby.' The baby has you."

—*Gallagher*

dialed ^{get} in

Between work and baby, you barely have time to breathe. This is when having a list of helpers programmed into your speed dial can save the day. Having this thought out in advance will transform you into a hero in your wife's eyes. Here, a primer:

when your wife says:	have this number handy:
"I'm starving and there's no food in the house."	Her favorite pizza or Chinese food delivery spot
"We're out of toilet paper."	Any grocery store that delivers
"My body aches and I need a break."	A masseuse who makes house calls
"I never have any time alone."	The local manicure/pedicure joint
"I can't take living in filth anymore."	A housekeeping service
"Who are you?"	A relative, family friend, or reputable babysitting service—and the best restaurant in town (make reservations first)

sitting
pretty

It was touch and go there for a while, but you powered through those treacherous first weeks and months. If you're lucky, your wife may even still be speaking to you. This is where it starts to get fun. Your child is now more baby than blob, and she's about to start learning all manner of exciting new **tricks**. One of the best? Sitting up. To help her master this milestone, prop her up with plenty of **pillows** or rolled-up towels (mom's breastfeeding pillow works great for this). Do this on a soft, carpeted square of floor—never on the couch, as a baby's relatively leaden head can pull her over *fast*.

gear
up

Guys like gear. You're a guy. So what are you waiting for? One of your many (implicit but irrevocable) jobs right now is to whip out the digital camera and camcorder on a regular basis. Score 10 bonus points if you catalog your photos in handy, easy-to-access files on your wife's computer, 20 if you send out a batch to family and friends without her having to ask, and 50 if you download the cutest shot to her phone or screensaver. (If you—gasp!—don't even *have* the equipment yet, put down this book and get to the mall. Time's ticking, and who knows what adorable milestone you're about to miss. You really can't be too careful here.)

It is **admirable** *for* a **man** to take his **son** fishing, but there is a *special* place in heaven for the father who takes his **daughter** shopping.

—John Sinor

this
sucks

When baby's crying and you're ready to pull out your last hair, try this: gently insert the tip of your (clean) pinkie finger into his mouth, padded side up. Suckling can be infinitely **soothing** to newborns—unless he happens to be hungry, in which case he could become furious when he discovers that there's no milk coming out. If that happens, you can feel confident it's time for a feeding.

clean up your act

You thought your wife gave you a hard time about your five o'clock shadow? If your baby could talk, he'd be *begging* you to shave. A full beard is fine—nobody is suggesting you overhaul your lifelong image here—but do you think two-day stubble feels fabulous against virgin skin? Likewise, your exquisitely macho man-hands won't cut it. Make yourself baby-friendly by keeping your cheeks closely shaven, your nails neatly trimmed, and your hands clean and smooth. This might even be an excuse to get one of those *man*-icures you've been curious about. It'll score major points with your partner as well (and your poker buddies will never need to know).

home
sweet
home

Every day when you come home from work you find the same thing: a belligerent baby and a manic mom. For some reason—probably a combination of his immature nervous system and irregular sleep patterns—the early evening, from about 5 to 7 p.m., tends to be rough for babies (and subsequently their parents). It's so common that it's even been unofficially dubbed "*the witching hour*," and it's probably no coincidence that it happens around cocktail hour. If your wife's been the primary caregiver all day, expect her to hand the cranky, cantankerous babe over to you and promptly disappear. Welcome to unhappy hour, dad. If **rocking** and **bouncing** don't soothe him, try stepping outside for a bit or putting him into a warm bath. Sometimes a simple change of scenery and temperature is enough to snap him out of it. Other times, of course, you just have to ride out the storm . . . and look forward to the beverage waiting for you once he's happily asleep.

* **Lie on your back** and tuck your knees to your chest, then place baby on your shins and hold her securely. Rock back and forth and make airplane noises. Eventually you can extend your legs and graduate to the full-blown rocket launch, but probably not until she can sit up solo.

* **Place her** on your chest and hold her securely as you do crunches. She won't realize her primary purpose is adding weight; she'll just enjoy the ride.

* **Enroll her in** infant swimming classes and tell your wife that this is your domain. She'll appreciate the hour-long break as well as the opportunity *not* to put on a swimsuit in public.

* **Make yourself into** a human swing, leaning over at your waist and creating a "seat" for baby's bottom with your hands. Swing arms gently back and forth.

* **Gently toss baby** up into the air and catch her. Do not do this on concrete or when your wife is at home, or even in the country. She will faint on the spot even though it is really fun and kids love it.

* **Bounce with her** on an exercise ball or minitrampoline (be sure to support her head and neck carefully).

* **Strap her into** a front carrier and take her for a lively stroll, complete with commentary and/or silly songs.

* **Play the** "I'm going to pretend to tickle you" game and see just how easily you can make her squirm.

* **Throw a** (preferably clean) burp cloth over your head and let the manic peekaboo marathon begin.

* **In a standing position**, hold one arm as if you were cupping a football to your ribcage and drape her over it, facedown. Cradling her head in your hand (and holding her body firmly with the other hand), rock her swiftly from side to side, with musical accompaniment.

Once she's mastered head and neck control:

* **Sit with one leg** crossed over the other, and hold her hands as she sits on the top, flexed foot. Gently kick your foot out and back, and watch as she enjoys her first pretend pony ride.

go ahead,
horse around

You watch as your wife gently, tenderly handles your precious cargo with caresses and whispers; meanwhile, you try to stymie your boyish urges to roughhouse and do loud, goofy impersonations. Don't! The truth is, it's crucial for your child to experience **both** forms of love and stimulation. Your wife will make sure the baby gets plenty of soft, warm nurturing, leaving you free to embrace your new role as designated horsey-ride giver, tummy tickler, and human play structure (complete with swing, climbing wall, and slide) all rolled into one. Yes, you have to be safe, but it can still be lots of fun. Here, how to get physical . . .

Until she can hold her head up solo:

* **Bicycle her legs** as she lies on her play mat (be prepared for gaseous emissions when you do this).

* **Entertain her** with exaggerated facial expressions as she enjoys tummy time (feel free to gesticulate widely, and stick out your tongue if this earns giggles or grins).

Cleaning your **house** while your **kids** are *still* **growing up** is like **shoveling** the walk **before** it stops **snowing**.

—Phyllis Diller

you can
take it with you

Mom's taking a much-needed nap, and you and junior are heading to the park. No matter how comfortable you are in your masculinity, you probably don't want to tote her pink paisley bag. And you don't need to! Best of all, your alternatives no longer consist of a grocery bag or gallon-size ziplock bag. Diaper bag manufacturers have gotten pretty savvy, offering up plenty of hip, he-man styles you won't feel totally goofy carrying around. Messenger bags are easy to find and the cross-gender rage, but if even that's too metrosexual for your tastes, a nice insulated backpack will hold all the necessary bells and whistles while still preserving your manly style. (Just don't forget to put some diapers and wipes in there, MacGyver.)

help!
my son has
moobs!

Your wife's suddenly ample bosom may be a welcome sight, but a noticeable pair of hooters on your baby can be downright disturbing. Don't be alarmed if your newborn son or daughter seems to be exhibiting extremely early prepubescence. These little "breast buds" (yes, that's a technical term) are a product of maternal hormones absorbed through the placenta. As his *own* hormone levels stabilize over the next few weeks, his moobs will disappear. Whew.

Dinner and a baby

Your baby will never be more portable than she is *right now*. Her cries also probably haven't escalated from paltry to piercing yet, which is a plus for activities such as restaurant dining. Strap her into her portable car seat and get thee to dinner. Believe it or not, the more bustling the atmosphere, the more likely she may be to fall asleep in the middle of it all. Even if she stays wide awake, the festival of new sights and sounds is sure to delight and amuse her long enough for you and your lovely wife to shovel in some grub—with no dishes to contend with later.

A **father** is *someone* who carries
pictures in
his **wallet** where his
money used to be.

—*Unknown*

if he's:	try:	because:
fussy & colicky	the football hold	Cradling him facedown over your forearm (use your hand to support his head, with his arms and legs on either side of your arm, like an airplane) may help relieve gas pressure—plus it gives him a new perspective.
sleepy	the cradle hold	This traditional faceup, rock-a-bye move (with the back of his head nestled into the crook of your arm) allows eye contact—great for rocking and singing him to sleep.
bored	the shoulder hold	Propping him up allows him to see a whole new world over your shoulder. Do it by cradling his chest to your shoulder, wrapping one arm below his bottom, and using the other to hold his upper back snugly.
curious	the outward hold	He wants to know where he's going, too. Place his back against your chest, wrapping one arm around his front and the other beneath his bottom; it's a great hold for deep knee bends or exercise-ball bouncing.

hold it
right there

First things first: you will *not* break the baby simply by picking him up. (Dropping him is another story altogether.) How best to cradle your little **dumpling**? That depends on his mood, so don't get stuck endlessly using one position. Dads, with their stronger arms and generally more **adventurous** spirit, are notoriously good at attempting new holds. Try these and you might just be able to soothe junior faster than mom.

pardon you!

Your little angel is downing liquid by the gallon—and now she's got more gas than Exxon. Fortunately most guys like clear, specific tasks, and this one has your name all over it. After your baby is finished feeding, confidently lift her into your arms and announce, "I got it from here." The key to successfully releasing trapped air from that tiny tummy is to apply just enough—but not too much—pressure to the area. Grab a dish towel or burp cloth or 8 x 10 foot tarp and cover the vicinity below your baby's mouth (burping is not a dry endeavor). Then either lay the baby across your lap so that your thighs are gently pressing into her abdomen, or lift her high onto your shoulder until she can just peek over it. Then pat her back gently until she burps up the goods. Generally speaking, the more expensive and freshly laundered your own clothing, the quicker and more successful you will be.

Work it out

So mom's not the only one who's been hitting the chocolate sauce? Those extra few (or forty) pounds are known as "sympathy weight gain," a phenomenon that afflicts the fittest of fathers. As impossible—and selfish—as it might feel to sneak away for a workout, it'll be good for everyone concerned. You could try to find a nearby slope and do some stroller-sprints, which would benefit both you *and* baby. But don't forget you need some alone time, too—as well as some one-on-one time with your wife. If a solo sweat session doesn't sound appealing, think of a pastime you two used to love to do together—rollerblading, tennis, a beach stroll, horseshoes—and schedule an activity date with her. Start with something manageable, like a one-hour walk. Get one of the grandmas to watch junior and it's a triple win. No next of kin in proximity? Craigslist and local nanny agencies are teeming with able-bodied babysitters. Taking the initiative to interview a few of them to have on file will score major points with your partner. (Whatever you do, don't hire the suntanned summering supermodel, even if she is a pediatric paramedic, okay? Your wife will *not* be amused or impressed.)

ten *comments*
that **could**
save your
marriage

1. Dinner's ready!
2. I'll get up with the baby tonight.
3. I can't believe how quickly that baby weight is falling off of you!
4. All of the laundry is folded and put away.
5. I didn't think I could love you more, but I was wrong.
6. We were both bottle-fed, and we turned out just fine.
7. I hope you don't mind that I scheduled a massage for you.
8. Our baby is lucky to have you for a mom.
9. Let me hold him while you take a bubble bath.
10. I just want to cuddle you.*

*It is best if this is said with a sincere face and strict follow-through

ten *questions* **not** to ask your wife right now

1. How'd you sleep last night?
2. Why won't she stop crying?
3. What's for dinner?
4. Are you sure he's getting enough to eat?
5. Did you want my mom to stay for one month or two?
6. When do you think you'll lose that weight?
7. Okay if I go out with the guys again tonight?
8. Did you wear those pajamas all day?
9. You feeling frisky?
10. What were we *thinking*?

fun
parenting facts!*

105 — The number of boys born for every 100 girls

$7,000 — Total spent on baby items before his first birthday

22 lb 8 oz — Heaviest birth weight on record ("It's a BIG boy!")

$242,070 — Cost of raising a child to 18 (not including college)

500 years — Time it takes for one disposable diaper to decompose

9 million — Number of people in the world who share your baby's birthday

*Source: happyworker.com

say
cheese!

Somewhere around the six-week mark, it will happen. Your baby will burst into the goofiest, most **heartbreakingly beautiful** grin you have ever seen in your life. (And then you'll know all of those *other* grins you thought you may have seen were, alas, gas.) The First Smile may or may not be in response to any particular action on your part, but that is immaterial. For the next several days/weeks/ months, you will repeatedly do whatever you happened to be doing when the magical reaction transpired—tickling her tummy, sing-ing "Yankee Doodle Dandy," bonking yourself on the head with a sledgehammer—in the hopes of seeing it again. With any luck, she'll cooperate before you sustain a major brain injury. Go for it!

"You can learn
many things from children.
How much
patience you have,
for instance."

—Franklin P. Jones

To be a successful father,
there's one absolute rule:
when you have a kid,
don't look at it
for the first two years.

—Ernest Hemingway

* **You look** exactly like . . .

* Today when **you were asleep** on my chest and I was watching the news/quarterfinals/clock tick, I was thinking . . .

* Right now, the **most important thing** in my life is . . .

* It **cracks me up** when you . . .

* **I can't wait** until you're old enough for us to . . .

* After **you win** the Pulitzer Prize, I hope you'll still remember . . .

Note: Always date your entries! You will enjoy looking back on these in years to come, and besides, the time frame will help explain any grammar and spelling errors or incomprehensible scribbles.

write
now!

Statistically speaking, there's a good chance your partner has appointed herself family historian. As she diligently records your newborn's every coo in an heirloom-style baby book (or at least threatens to), what's a guy to do? Start your own keepsake journal. It doesn't have to be fancy—a nice spiral-bound, college-rule notebook will do just fine (and frankly, can remove some of the pressure to be perfect). Jot down funny feeding moments and disastrous diapering episodes, describe a wonderful day or moment together, or simply confess your undying affection. Wouldn't it be amazing to read this kind of simple love letter from your dad? Some ideas to help you get pen to paper:

* The first time I held you in my arms I thought . . .

* My greatest wish for you is . . .

* When I think about the day you were born, I will always remember . . .

tube
time

Everyone knows that plunking your kid in front of the idiot box for hours on end is not healthy or wise. But in the early days, many babies can be soothed by the rhythmic hum of, say, a soccer match or football game playing softly in the background. (And it's not like she can even see as far as the screen, so there's no need to worry about your chosen sport's potentially violent nature—yet.) We're not saying your wife will like or even approve of your tandem TV time, but chances are, if it means a break for her, she'll cave. If you're planning a double nap, hunker down on the couch or recliner until you're perfectly horizontal and place baby on your chest, preferably skin-on-skin, with a cozy blankie within arm's reach. Sweet dreams.

boot
up

Even though you knew it was coming (your wife's continually growing belly was kinda hard to miss, after all), you didn't know it would be quite like *this*. Lots of new dads feel overwhelmed by their unfamiliar roles, which is why you should go out of your way to meet them and compare war stories. Now, look: we know the whole touchy-feely "let's talk about how this makes us *feel*" stuff generally makes men **cringe**. But today's guy groups, like Boot Camp for New Dads (www.bootcampfornewdads.org), understand that and go to great lengths to give their seminars a macho feel. You'll have fun, get inspired, and leave with a heaping dose of confidence—the only thing you may be lacking in the dad department. Other options include finding a local parenting group that you can join with your mate (ask your pediatrician or check online), or just organizing a monthly get-together with friends or co-workers who are new dads.

The **most important** thing a **father** can **do** for his **children** is to **love** their *mother*.

—Rev. Theodore Hesburgh

you
rock

Babies thrive on familiarity. Here's how you can help: create a playlist of her favorite tunes thus far, then either burn it onto a CD or download it to your iPod. Your musical masterpiece will come in handy not just at home but in the **car**, as well as on overnight **trips** to just about anywhere. Insider tip: if you go the CD route and plan to use it during naps, make sure to hit the repeat button before tiptoeing from the room; otherwise the sudden silence at the end could wake her.

to do it every day, especially in the beginning. Sponge baths (read: wiping her down quickly with a warm washcloth before pj's go on, probably the routine you've been doing yourself) are a fine alternative at least every other day.

it's a
wash

Once the umbilical cord falls off, you get the green light to give baby a real bath. The first thing you'll notice when you do this is that babies are really, *really* slippery when wet. You also may notice that in proportion to your bathtub, she is extremely small. You can either purchase an infant tub that sits on a counter or inside your bigger tub, or simply bathe her in the kitchen sink. Make sure you clean out the sink really well in advance, clear off the counter, and have all the necessities nearby before you start: a clean diaper, dry towel, two washcloths (one to wash her and one to drape over the exposed parts of her wet body to keep her warm), pajamas or a change of clothes, and a mild cleanser. A note about the cleanser: since you will be holding the baby at any given moment with at least one hand but possibly two, it's wise either to enlist help when bathing her, or to pretreat your washcloth with a dollop before you begin the process. Never submerge her all the way, always support her head, and make sure to do a thorough job in and around her neck folds, where milk tends to collect. Don't worry; this—along with most other parenting tasks—gets a lot easier. And the good news is, there's no need

"By the time a man *realizes* that *maybe* his **father** *was* right, he usually **has a son** who thinks *he's* **wrong**."

—*Charles Wadsworth*

"Never raise *your hand* to your kids. It leaves *your* groin unprotected."

—*Red Buttons*

no idea what you're doing. That's the nature of this wacky time in your life. Confused and frustrated? Excellent! Tired and cranky? Bravo! You're right on track. Think of early fatherhood like a fraternity hazing ritual: everyone has to go through it, and in the end they emerge stronger, closer, and not noticeably worse for the wear. Welcome to the club!

dazed and confused?

Whoever decided that the Peace Corps was the "toughest job you'll ever love" obviously didn't have kids. Suddenly, trudging to the office—ten miles each way, uphill in the snow—and toiling away there until the wee hours of the night seems like a trip to adult Disneyland. The truth is, with this gig some hours will drag, some will pass in a blur. One minute you'll feel like Superdad, the next you'll be convinced you're a bumbling failure. Some days will be delightful from dawn to dusk, and others will rank just below an IRS audit on the fun scale. The partner you love and adore, the one with whom you created a human life, may look you in the eye and tell you that she hates you. (Relax. She doesn't hate you. She hates the fact that she hasn't slept in months and that her body is leaking from multiple locations.) You will laugh and cry, sometimes in the same hour but possibly even at the same time. You're not depressed, you're not bipolar, and you're not a bad dad. You're exhausted and you have

It *doesn't* **matter** who my **father** was; it matters who **I remember** **he** was.

—*Anne Sexton*

zip-a-de-do,
dad!

A little-known fact*: the term **snaps**, when used to express congratulations, was coined the day the first bleary-eyed dad managed to secure sixteen of the buggers—in the right order, without missing a single one—in the middle of the night up a flailing infant's legs. The dim-wit who designed this garment calamity ought to be hog-tied. **Zippers**, pal. It's all about zippers. Do yourself and your baby's mother a huge favor and stockpile only those pj's that zip up the front, or gowns with no fasteners at all. Your fingers will thank you.

*Because it's not technically true although it should be

doody
calls

Dealing with the first few messy diapers can be daunting (even though, luckily, newborn number two isn't terribly putrid). You'll look like a seasoned pro if you master a few simple tricks to make the process smoother. First, open a clean diaper and slide it into position underneath his body (as if he were naked) before you begin. Next, unhook the tabs from the dirty diaper and use the inside front to make one giant sweep from front to back while holding up his ankles. Continue all the way around until the diaper is folded in half underneath the baby, so he's sitting on top of the (clean) front. Use as many wipes as necessary—always wiping front to back—until all of his many folds and crevices are poop-free. Place these on top of the dirty diaper, and then pull the whole pile out from under him. Fold the bottommost part up and then secure the tabs around it, creating a nice, neat, burrito-style package. Doing this will keep your hands cleaner, minimize any scent leakage, and also prevent the tabs from sticking to (and invariably ripping) the inside of the diaper pail liner. He may, of course, choose this time to add some moisture to the mix; the diaper below him will—with any luck—catch those drippings. See how smart you are?

Midnight madness

"But I have to get up and go to work in the morning!" This battle cry won't cut it during the first few weeks. Mom's got a tough job right now, too. Taking responsibility for a midnight feeding or two will score major marital points. Even if your wife is nursing, you can still retrieve and change the baby for her and make sure she has a huge glass of water within reach. You can't imagine how much your partner will appreciate this show of solidarity.

HAPPY PARENTS
make
HAPPY BABIES

sleep:
what's that again?

Concert T-shirts, a closet to yourself, plaid flannel sheets, five uninterrupted hours of sleep: ah, yes, all things you *used* to have. Now when someone tells you they slept like a baby last night, you'd bet your last nickel they don't have one. You see, it takes a while for babies' internal clocks to develop, so they tend to doze only at the most inopportune times (relative to, say, day and night). They also have stomachs roughly the size of ping-pong balls, so they need to eat way more frequently than you do. During those dark and peaceful stretches when you used to be happily impersonating a buzz saw, be prepared to be awakened—assuming you can fall asleep in the first place—at one- to three-hour intervals. Although this torture-chamber-style dream disruption won't last forever, it's best to go Zen for the duration and not try to fight it. You're probably at least half-awake even if mom's on nursing duty, so snuggle up with them and savor those quiet midnight cuddles. Memorize your baby's tiny, perfect features. Commit her delicious new-person scent to memory. These days will be gone before you know it and—as crazy as this might sound right now—one day you'll pine for them.

cutting
the cord

The umbilical cord is a wondrous thing, isn't it? For the better part of a year, it was the tether that connected your child to his or her mother. It provided a steady stream of food and nutrients without even being asked! Once that vital cord has been snipped, however, its striking resemblance to dehydrated meat is enough to turn you off beef jerky forever. The crusty little stump will fall off on its own, usually within the first two to three weeks of your baby's life. Until then, fold diapers down and away to minimize irritation, **follow** your pediatrician's **advice** for cleaning it (most insist plain old water is fine), and whatever you do, don't tug at it. During routine cleaning it may bleed a bit; this is normal and not cause for alarm. (Of course you *will* feel alarm if you see blood on your child, but it helps to remember that a little spotting is not dangerous or a sign of complications.) The upside: as long as the stump is still attached, you get to put off the first full submersion; for now you're on the sponge-bath plan.

in case you were
wondering...

* You *won't* break the baby.

* You *will* have sex again.

* You *did* put the crib together properly.

* You *will* be able to support your family.

* You *can* handle the responsibility.

* Your dog *will* get over it.

* You *are* the baby's real father.

* You *aren't* your father.

excuse me, doctor, but this can't be my baby

You've seen enough medical shows on TV to know what a newborn baby is supposed to look like. (Hint: not at *all* like the furry blue prune they just handed you.) Are you ready for a news flash? Those pretty pink prime-time babies are probably at least three to four months old. Why? Because newborn babies, to be frank, aren't the most attractive bunch. They often have lopsided, squished-in faces (from all that in utero yoga), gigantic cone-shaped heads (especially if they were delivered vaginally), and a full-body coating of fine hair (which can be especially dense on ears and bottom) that—thankfully—will disappear in a few short weeks. So don't worry if your initial reaction is to think that your offspring, though utterly wonderful, looks a little bit like an alien, or a monkey, or an alien monkey. This too shall pass.

right now; look for the *Happy Parents Make Happy Babies* icon for helpful tips on taking care of your partner *and* yourself during this life-altering time:

HAPPY PARENTS
make
HAPPY BABIES

So, first things first. Relax, breathe easy, and take it one day at a time. Remember, lesser men have made it through baby boot camp and lived to tell the tale, and you will, too. As impossible as it seems, before long, you're going to be the expert, the one all the other guys are coming to for advice, a father figure in every sense of the word. Pretty cool, huh?

Cheers, dad.

If you're like most guys, your dad-fantasies have probably focused mostly on those things that are still relatively far off: coaching the Little League team, climbing Mount Whitney together, terrorizing her dates as you polish the shotgun you don't technically own. But rest assured that in the meantime, there will be a million or more opportunities to interact and bond with your tot—just in the first year. *You'll burp, bathe, bounce, swaddle, entertain, feed, sing, soothe, and change enough diapers for a landfill as big as Texas.* Some of it will come naturally; other tasks (clipping fingernails comes to mind) can make even the most macho of men go weak in the knees. But you'll learn a lot along the way, both about the baby and about yourself.

A suggestion: When you're not sure how to do something, solicit your wife's input at your own peril. You see, at some moments, she might be happy to offer advice; at others, she'll just want to throttle you. (She's a bubbling cauldron of hormones right now and—trust us on this one—she'd really appreciate it if you found at least a few of your own answers.) Instead, sneak into the bathroom and skim through this book. It's jam-packed with tips and tricks you could certainly live without—you just wouldn't want to. And just imagine impressing your mate with some clever, successfully executed baby maneuvers! Also peppered throughout are friendly reminders that your newborn baby isn't the only one who needs tons of TLC

It *sometimes* happens, even in the best of families, that a baby is born. This is not *necessarily* cause for alarm. The important thing is to keep your wits about you and borrow some money.

—*Elinor Goulding Smith*

I won't **lie** to you,
fatherhood isn't *easy*
like **motherhood**.

—Homer Simpson

The truth is, raising a baby is an art, not a science. (If it was a science, there would be just one official how-to book and you'd be sitting here reading about boring, placebo-controlled studies.) And art, as you know, is subjective. And deeply personal. And very, very messy. Luckily, you're probably pretty good at messy.

You know that adorably dazed creature you brought home from the hospital? Well, she needs a lot of love, affection, and attention right now. So does the baby. You could probably use a little support yourself. Your mission for the next few months—and you really have no choice at this point but to accept it—is to keep everyone in the house alive, well, fed, clothed, and as happy and sane as humanly possible. No one said the job was going to be easy, and the pay is admittedly abysmal, but the perks have kept men coming back to the job since the beginning of time.

If the new American father feels *bewildered* and even **defeated**, let him take comfort from the **fact** that **whatever** he does in any **fathering situation** has a fifty percent **chance** of being right.

—*Bill Cosby*

However, you didn't get a play-book. And the coach is a girl. And your uniform is a little tight (because you're a giver and you couldn't have your partner gaining that pesky weight all by her little old self). And the other team is awfully scrawny and squirmy and, well, *fragile*. Fortunately, looks can be deceiving. Babies are hardy little things. What's more, they rank even higher than you do on the rookie scale, so they're not likely to bust you for winging it, messing up, or making up the rules as you go (at least not until they learn how to talk).

It is **much easier**

to **become** a *father*

than to **be** one.

—*Kent Nerburn*

you did it!

Can you believe it? You're a dad. Even though you knew it was coming, it still feels pretty amazing to see it and to say it, doesn't it? *Your boys can swim.* You survived (her) morning sickness. You managed to stay upright in the delivery room. Best of all, you now know best!

You have to admit that up until this point, your part in the whole reproduction process has been pretty minimal (not to mention fairly enjoyable). While your pregnant partner was groaning and growing, worrying and scurrying, your sole responsibility was to reassure her that everything was going to be fine, and occasionally to run to the store for more pickles/peaches/chocolate-covered Pringles. Look alive, dads: after months of waiting on the bench it's finally game time—and this time around you're first string.

About the Author

Renée Vernon

Jenna McCarthy is an internationally published writer whose work has appeared in more than forty magazines, on dozens of Web sites, and in several anthologies. The author of *The Parent Trip: From High Heels and Parties to Highchairs and Potties*, Jenna lives in Santa Barbara, California, with her husband, two daughters, three cats, and a dog. In her spare time, she wonders what she used to do with all of her spare time. Please visit her online at www.jennamccarthy.com.

cheers to the new
dad!

*tips & tricks to help
you ace the first months
of parenthood*

Jenna McCarthy

SASQUATCH BOOKS
SEATTLE

QUICK
& EASY massage

DUNCAN BAIRD PUBLISHERS

LONDON

QUICK
&EASY massage

Beata Aleksandrowicz

5-minute massages for

anyone

anytime

anywhere

QUICK
&EASY massage

Beata Aleksandrowicz

First published in the United Kingdom and Ireland in 2008 by
Duncan Baird Publishers Ltd
Sixth Floor
Castle House
75–76 Wells Street
London WIT 3QH

Conceived, created and designed by Duncan Baird Publishers

Copyright © Duncan Baird Publishers 2008
Text copyright © Beata Aleksandrowicz 2008
Photography copyright © Duncan Baird Publishers 2008

The right of Beata Aleksandrowicz to be identified as the Author of this
text has been asserted in accordance with the Copyright, Designs and
Patents Act of 1988.

Managing Editor: Grace Cheetham
Editor: Judith More
Managing Designer: Manisha Patel
Designer: Jantje Doughty
Commissioned photography: Jules Selmes

British Library Cataloguing-in-Publication Data:
A CIP record for this book is available from the British Library

ISBN: 978-1-84483-580-5

10 9 8 7 6 5 4 3 2 1

Typeset in Gill Sans, Nofret and Helvetica Neue
Colour reproduction by Scanhouse, Malaysia
Printed in China by Imago

Publisher's notes: The information in this book is not intended as a
substitute for professional medical advice and treatment. If you are
pregnant or are suffering from any medical conditions or health problems,
it is recommended that you consult a medical professional before
following any of the advice or practice suggested in this book. Duncan
Baird Publishers, or any other persons who have been involved in
working on this publication, cannot accept responsibility for any injuries
or damage incurred as a result of following the information, exercises or
therapeutic techniques contained in this book.

To my Mum and my Dad
– who loved me as much
as they could

contents

6 introduction

anytime

22 morning wake-up
24 shower time
26 lunchtime lift
28 evening de-stress
30 lazy weekend
32 take a moment
34 before a meeting
36 at a conference

anywhere

40 in your bedroom
42 in your bathroom
44 on your sofa
46 at the park
48 at the beach
50 at your desk
52 in a hotel room
54 on a plane

stress busters

58 scalp lifter
60 lower back reliever
62 body relaxer
64 eye calmer
66 jaw reliever
68 foot de-stresser
70 neck balancer

mood enhancers

74 chest booster
76 foot reviver
78 face lifter
80 abdominal soother
82 head booster
84 neck warmer
86 sinus clearer

energy boosters

90 shoulder stretcher
92 face booster
94 neck reviver
96 thigh booster
98 ear reviver
100 back releaser
102 body energizer

practising together

106 getting connected
108 letting go
110 back relaxer
112 working together
114 sleep enhancer
116 touching hands
118 caring for feet
120 balancing touch
122 tension reliever

124 everyday sequences

126 index/acknowledgments

introduction

This is a book for everybody – whatever your age, you will enjoy the proven healing benefits of all the massage sequences included and find the step-by-step approach easy to follow. All the techniques I share with you in this book are simple, yet these short rituals can make a big difference to your life, because they give you tools to reach out to others. Through touch, we communicate.

the healing touch

It was such a joy for me to work on this project because I strongly believe in the importance of massage in daily life – massage is so much more than just a once-a-year pampering treatment in a spa. Touch, the mother of all senses, can not only heal the aches and pains in our bodies caused by physical activities or stress, but also nourish our souls when we feel lonely, anxious, depressed or hurt.

In my everyday work, I experience the instant, often significant and wide-ranging effects, of massage. Based on the feedback from my clients, I know that massage doesn't just alleviate physical pain. After receiving a massage, my clients also feel more relaxed, positive, respected, appreciated and uplifted.

The physiological benefits of massage are well-known: muscles are toned and firmer, posture improves, the nervous system is more

6

balanced, the respiratory system is strengthened, the hormonal system is rebalanced, blood circulation is increased, and the skin is smoother and firmer. Massage encourages the lymph flow, which carries all waste products from the body so we can function more healthily, our immune system is strengthened, and our energy level lifts.

In my practice, I don't associate massage with pampering and all the luxury paraphernalia that it has been linked to in recent times. From its earliest inception, massage was intended as a healing art. Children in pain understand this instinctively: they come to their parents to soothe their hurt and we give them a little rub and a good word to make them feel better. Last century, nurses massaged soldiers to ease the wounds of war. And today, seriously ill patients, including AIDS and cancer sufferers, benefit from massage. Massage treatment reduces anxiety by helping to slow down the heart rate and relieve stress. It also reduces pain by releasing the well-being hormone, seratonin, and providing emotional comfort.

Touch is also a very powerful communication tool. I experienced this during a visit to the bushmen of the Kalahari Desert, in Namibia. I was among people who didn't speak my language, whose lives were completely different to mine, and yet we were able to create deep, profound contact through touch.

7

On the massage courses I run, I often tell participants that if they have an emotional moment when they don't know what to say, they should use touch instead. For example, just a light touch on the arm or hand will bring much-needed comfort and a feeling of support to a bereaved person, when words may not flow easily.

who benefits from massage?

This book takes you through different situations in everyday life where you can use massage – either on yourself, or to help a partner, child, parent or friend – to relieve physical and emotional tension.

The educational aspect of the book is very important to me as I believe that massage can be taught to everybody, and more importantly can be used in every moment of our hectic lives. As recent research studies show, general stress levels are rising, making a healing touch a daily necessity.

In the baby massage course I run, I have observed how crying babies respond positively to touch, and calm down. Recent studies have shown that babies develop faster, and that their mothers develop better communication with them, if they are massaged regularly.

For seniors, too, I believe that touch is crucial as they can feel rejected, or embarrassed by their age and the changes that have

taken place in their bodies. I am convinced that if you can give your grandmother or grandfather, or your mother or father, a soothing neck or a hand massage, it can make a world of difference in their life.

With teenagers, who generally avoid any sort of communication, massage can be a way for another member of the family to listen to their emotions, and soothe their pains.

And for couples, a simple foot or hand massage at bedtime is a caring gesture that builds trust and understanding. It is a wonderful non-verbal expression of their bond, and will reassure both partners that they are important to each other.

I want this book to help you to believe in yourself, and in your abilities to massage. In its pages I set out to show you that you don't have to be vulnerable when confrontating physical or emotional pain, and to teach you how you can help yourself and others using this time-honoured, natural self-healing method.

I also would like to encourage you to share your touch with others. To help you to achieve this I have created a final chapter that includes "each-other" massage techniques. If you follow the instructions in this chapter, and you trust in yourself, you can master these techniques and share them with others. Massage is such a great way to communicate with those you share your life with.

The techniques in chapter 6 can be shared between husband and wife, children and parents, or friends. They give you a chance to communicate through touch, and teach you helpful massage sequences you can use to express caring feelings to all those who are close to you. You should always try to give your massage partner the best massage you can, and never refuse to give one – for tomorrow it might be you who will be asking for a much-needed healing touch.

Be aware that massage is a giving and receiving process, and from my experience there is an equal distribution of energy between the giver and the receiver. Therefore, you should always try to exchange massages equally. That said, however, it is a good habit to agree that the person who is more tense or tired should receive their massage first. The reason for this lies in the fact that we transmit all our emotions and thoughts with our touch, therefore it is important that your mind is relaxed, and is filled with positive thoughts and emotions, while you are offering massage to somebody. else

Massage is of great benefit to most people. However, there are some cases where it is not appropriate. For a list of the basic contra-indications you must take into account before you start any massage, see the list on pages 13–14. If in doubt, I would recommend that you ask your general practitioner if massage is suitable for you.

contra-indications

If you fall into one of these categories you should avoid massage:

- You have a high temperature. Massage stimulates the body's metabolism, and can cause the temperature to rise even higher. You can still use touch of course! We all know the blissful sensation of somebody's cold hand on our forehead when we are sick.

- It is less than an hour since you ate a large meal. Don't use massage techniques on a full stomach, to prevent pressure on inner organs.

- You have had a recent injury or an accident that caused open wounds, bruising, or fractures. In such cases, you should always take professional advice before embarking on a massage.

- You have a serious lower back problem, persistent back or neck pain, or any other significant body restriction. If this is the case, you should go to an osteopath to check out the cause of the problem and discuss massage options with him or her.

- You are pregnant. If you are pregnant, you should massage your lower back and abdomen very gently during the first three months. You must also take professional advice regarding the oils you use, as some essential oils are unsuitable for pregnant women.

- If you have varicose veins, avoid any direct pressure on affected veins, and keep any pressure very light around such an area.

a time and a place

You may wonder how it's possible to find time for even a simple, short massage. We all need more time, and most of us think that our day is too short. We often postpone time for ourselves —"me-time" – to the following day. To solve this problem, I have based the massage treatments in this book around natural breaks that you can find in your everyday activities. Your quick-and-easy massage session won't interfere with your day in any way, but rather give you strength, and enable you to enjoy your free time in a more relaxed manner.

I've suggested ideas for using massage techniques in almost every circumstance: during a long flight, in the shower, at your desk, or resting on the beach. You will also find techniques that will help you to release stress or add energy to your life, or help you to enhance your mood. You can use this book anytime and anywhere: at home, in the office, at the hospital. My aim is to prove that you can use massage in everyday life. You don't need any special preparation, and you don't have to be a qualified massage therapist to soothe neck pain, or to comfort your loved one. On the other hand, it is important to say that the book is not a replacement for professional massage.

My wish is also to show you that you don't have to feel powerless when confronting pain – your own or another's. You can help your body and your mind in the most ancient and natural way. If you don't know what to say, or do, then just touch.

golden rules

There are some key rules to follow if you want to get the maximum benefit from this book. Please read these carefully before you begin.

- **Breathing well.** You should regard breathing as an internal massage of all your organs. When you take an in-breath, your lungs expand, pushing on the diaphragm, which causes a cascade effect on all the organs below, including your stomach, liver, and kidneys. This happens because they are all attached to each other through the connective tissue, therefore whatever movement takes place in one organ, the others are affected. Breathing fills your lungs with oxygen, which is then transferred to your blood cells, and these carry the oxygen around your body. Very often, feelings of fatigue, headaches, impaired vision, and poor motor coordination are caused by incorrect breathing.

- **Staying silent.** It is important that you don't talk during massage. That way, you can switch off your mind, as a kind of mental break, refreshing your whole system. Some of the techniques in this book can be carried out at home, where it is obviously easier to follow the rule of silence. If you are in a public place, you'll need to be

15

more disciplined in order to switch off and tune in with yourself. Use deep, regular breathing as your guide. Concentrate purely on your breathing for two or three minutes before you start self-massage, to help you to switch off your mind.

- **Getting the pressure right.** If you listen to your body carefully, it will tell you if the pressure is wrong. Pain usually signifies that you are using pressure that is too strong or too fast. Lighten up immediately, and slow the movement down. Apply pressure gradually, rather than pushing suddenly. In all techniques that require static pressure, trust your intuition to locate the sore spots. With practice, you will become more and more aware of the tension that is always present in a sore spot as a result of the build-up of waste products (mostly toxins that haven't been removed by the circulation). Avoid direct pressure on the bones, especially when you are working along the spine. Always concentrate pressure on the muscles.

- **Finding the right rhythm and speed.** Practice making slow movements. Imagine that you are walking through a city that you have never seen before. If you run, you can't experience anything fully. You need time and awareness to assimilate as much as possible from an unknown place. The same is true of the human body. Discover it slowly and carefully through the process of touch. The more

you are present, the more natural the slow speed of massage will become. Keep a steady rhythm as you work, and make at least as many repetitions as I have suggested in the book. By making these rhythmical, repetitive movements you are helping your nervous system to relax and restore the natural balance of your body.

how to use this book

You can start to try massage from any page: the book is structured in such a way that it is easy for you to use every day. I have made sure that all the techniques featured are simple enough for beginners. All you need is your desire to connect with yourself, or with the other person you will be massaging. Always begin by breathing deeply several times, with closed eyes, to relax both body and mind.

I believe that this book will become your trusty companion, not only as a source of remedies for aches and pains, but also because it can make every moment in your life a bit more meaningful through the transforming power of touch. I hope that by using this book you will become as passionate about massage as I am, and that this book will bring joy into your life – the joy of giving and receiving touch.

19

anytime

You can put massage techniques to work at any convenient moment to release tension and make you feel better. In the morning, massage is a great preparation for the challenges of the day, while in the evening there is no better way to relax both body and mind.

1 Sit on the side of the bed, with your feet touching the floor. Relax your arms and make sure that you have a good connection between your feet and the surface underneath. Place your hands on your lap and close your eyes. Take a deep, slow breath. Gently, without any force, breathe out. Repeat three times.

2 (*right*) Put your right hand on your scalp, while the left one rests on your lap. Comb your fingers through the roots of your hair, close to the forehead, and close your fist. Grasp as much hair as you can, take a deep breath and, while breathing out, pull gently on the hair. Keep your fist very close to your scalp. Release.

3 While taking another in-breath, reposition your right hand toward the back of your scalp, grasp as much hair as you can, and pull gently with the out-breath. Continue pulling and releasing hair over the whole right side of your scalp. Pull firmly and rhythmically, so you can feel your scalp move. Use your left hand to work on the left side of your scalp.

4 Place the fingers of both hands on your head and tap gently all over the scalp, breathing regularly. Imagine that heavy rain drops are falling on your head. Increase the speed of the tapping motion until you feel a pleasant warmth spreading all over your scalp. If you prefer, you can use relaxed fists, tapping gently, as an alternative to your fingers.

morning wake-up
invigorating

awaken physically and mentally when
you haven't had enough sleep

shower time
connecting

an ideal time to give yourself a very effective massage

1 Make sure that the water is hot enough to make you feel warm. Before you apply soap, stand quietly under the shower and feel the water pouring over your body, massaging it gently. Close your eyes, breathe deeply, and enjoy this very relaxing and soothing sensation.

2 Apply soap over your arms, shoulders, chest and neck, working up a lather. Make both your hands into loose fists, and start to roll your knuckles over your chest. The soap will encourage your fingers to slide without any resistance. Take care to avoid your collarbone, and work just on the chest area below it.

3 Place your right hand on your left arm at the elbow and make invigorating circles, sliding your hand up your arm. When you reach the shoulder, slide back down your arm to the elbow in one movement. Repeat three times, then make five energetic circles on your left shoulder. Change hands, then massage the opposite arm and shoulder in the same way.

4 (*opposite*) Make loose fists with both hands, and place them on the base of your neck. Roll your knuckles along the base of your neck, then up both sides to the base of your scalp. Come back to your starting point, knuckling the back of your neck from the base of the scalp down to the shoulders. Repeat three times. Finish the shower with lukewarm water.

25

1 Sit comfortably, with your feet touching the floor, and close your eyes. If you prefer to stand, relax your shoulders and don't lock your knees. Breathe deeply and regularly, concentrating on your breathing, to energize your body, and also give your mind a quick rest.

2 (*right*) Very slowly, lift your shoulders as high as you can, keeping your arms straight and loose. Do this gradually, with your in-breath. Any resistance in your shoulders will decrease with more repetitions. Don't force the movement, and lift only as high as is comfortable for you.

3 Hold your shoulders as high as possible for two slow in-breaths. With an out-breath, very slowly slide them down as low as you can, trying not to push, but rather releasing the muscles. Repeat three times. Each time, more space will open up between your shoulders and neck.

4 Place your right hand on your left shoulder socket, take an in-breath, and, while breathing out. rotate your hand inward over the socket, using fast, rhythmical movements. Breathe in again, then, while breathing out, make five outward rotations over the socket.

Change hands, and repeat this fast, rhythmical circling with your left hand over your right shoulder. Open your eyes, and breathe deeply.

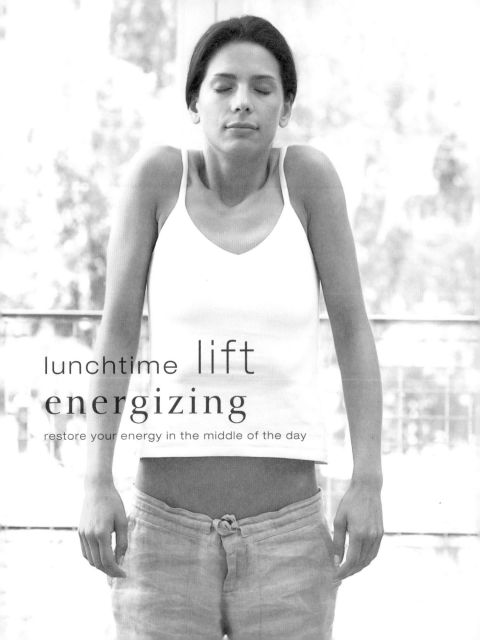

lunchtime lift
energizing
restore your energy in the middle of the day

evening de-stress
soothing

a great way to finish the day and improve your sleeping pattern

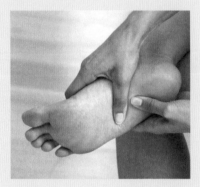

1 You can either sit on a chair or on the edge of the bed. Relax and rest your right foot on your left knee. Slowly and gently, apply cream to the top and sole of your foot. Sandwich your foot between your hands, and make circles with both hands all over the foot, starting from your toes and sliding toward your ankle.

2 Place both thumbs on the top of the sole, with fingers supporting the top of your foot. Press both thumbs into the sole and make three outward, deep, slow circles. Lift and move your thumbs to another point on your sole, press again, and make another three outward circles. Work all over sole and heel, taking care to breathe regularly.

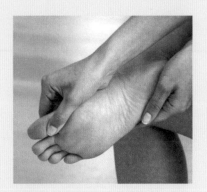

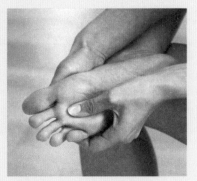

3 Cup your heel in the palm of your left hand for support. Press your right thumb into your big toe. Make five slow circles in both directions, working on the whole surface of your big toe. Move to each of your other toes in turn and repeat the circles.

4 Now supporting your foot with your right hand, press your left thumb into the middle, top point of the sole. Slide down along this middle line to the edge of your heel, using your left thumb. Hold your foot between both hands, breathing deeply three times. Finally, repeat the massage sequence in steps 1–4 on your left foot.

lazy weekend

pampering

relax your hands and leave them looking firm and fresh

1 Sit comfortably on the sofa, supporting your back with a pillow and keeping your legs straight, knees supported. Apply hand cream to the back and fingers of your right hand, using slow movements and covering the hand to the wrist. Stroke from fingers to wrist several times, then apply cream to your right palm.

2 (*opposite*) Rest your right hand on the fingers of your left hand, palm up. Using the thumb of your left hand, slide along the tendons, from the knuckle of your little finger toward the wrist. Repeat between every finger, working each time from the knuckle toward the wrist.

3 Squeeze the base of the little finger of your right hand between the thumb and index fingers of your left hand, and make circles around the finger, working up to the fingernail. Repeat on each finger three times, breathing slowly and keeping your shoulders relaxed.

4 Massage the palm of your right hand with the thumb of your left hand, using the fingers of the left hand as support. Make small circles with your thumb all over the palm. You should feel the tension releasing. Finish by holding both hands together and breathing deeply three times. Repeat steps 1–4 once more, this time on your other hand.

31

take a moment focusing

release tension, to leave you alert and refreshed

1 Standing in front of a mirror will help you to control the position of every movement. Start by taking three deep breaths. Stroke one hand after another up your forehead, into the hairline, five times. Relax your hands and make sure that the movement is slow, but rhythmical. Take care that you don't apply too much pressure.

2 Place the fingers of both hands over your forehead. Press slowly into the skin, using the finger pads, and make five outward, slow, regular circles. Try not to just stretch the skin – think about creating slow movements of the tissue underneath. Make sure that you cover the whole forehead, including the hairline and above the eyebrows.

3 Hold both your hands across your forehead and press in with the index and middle fingers. Make a "zig-zag" stroke, moving both hands toward each other. Start slowly, then gradually increase the speed, before slowing down again. Work all over the forehead for 30 seconds.

4 Place the ring and middle finger of your right hand on the bridge of your nose, between your eyebrows, and take an in-breath. Rest your left hand in your lap. Make light circles in a spiral movement, sliding along the middle line of the forehead from the base of the nose up to the hairline. Breathe deeply, keeping your shoulders relaxed.

33

before a meeting
balancing

energize and give yourself a sense of harmony

1 Place one hand on top of each shoulder, with palms facing down. Firmly embrace the muscles that lie on top of the shoulder and connect to the neck. Breathing out slowly, squeeze and lift your shoulders in your hands, and hold. On the next out-breath, release your grip slowly. Repeat three times, lifting and holding each time.

2 Form fists and place them on the top of each shoulder. On the out-breath, tap vigorously and rhythmically along the muscular part of your shoulders. Make sure that your hands don't slide onto the bone, which might be painful. Breathe regularly, and continue tapping for 15 seconds.

34

3 Gently place one hand on each shoulder, with your palms facing down. Close your eyes, and feel a comforting warmth emanating from your shoulders. Imagine "sending" your breath toward your shoulders.

4 Place one hand on either side of your head. On the out-breath, press gently into the scalp and hold. Breathe in. With another out-breath, release the pressure, feeling the warmth of your hands on your scalp. Repeat three times. Open your eyes.

55

1 Make sure that you are sitting straight, legs uncrossed and feet connecting with the floor. Take off your shoes if possible. Relax your shoulders and bend your neck slightly forward to reduce any tension in it. You need to be aware that if you bend your neck too much you will cause additional resistance, instead of helping your muscles to relax.

2 (*right*) Place your right hand on your left shoulder. Breathe deeply, feeling the hand's warmth spreading over the shoulder. Press your index and middle fingers into the muscle without changing position, and, with an out-breath, make as many slow, deep circles as you wish. If the spot is sore, press into the muscle and just hold for several breaths.

3 Work along the shoulder, selecting the most tender spots and massaging them using either circular or static pressure. Start with slow, deep circles, then increase the speed. With your left hand, work on the other shoulder, repeating steps 1–3.

4 Place both hands on your lap, bring your head back upright, and rotate your shoulders five times backward and five times forward, keeping your neck relaxed. Make sure that you don't bend your elbows or use your lower arms; you should feel the movement starting from the shoulder. Breathe deeply three times.

at a conference
refreshing

maintain your mind and body energy during demanding events

anywhere

You don't have to go to a spa to experience the benefits of massage.

You can apply simple techniques wherever you are, to help you relax,

to boost your energy, or to ease tension or minor pains.

in your bedroom
de-stressing

relax your lower back and relieve stress-related pain

1 Lie on your right side. Keeping your bottom leg straight, bend your upper leg and fold it over the bottom leg, so that the top ankle rests over the bottom knee. Rest your head on your right arm. You may be more comfortable if you put a small pillow or towel under your bent leg.

2 Place the palm of your left hand on your sacrum – the lowest part of your back where the spine connects with the buttocks. On the out-breath, gently press your palm into the sacrum. Release the pressure on the in-breath, then press in again with the next out-breath. Repeat the sequence until the whole area is nicely warmed up.

3 Start to massage your sacrum using the pads of your fingers. Work slowly and precisely, trying to release tension from every spot. Continue for several minutes. If anywhere is sore, roll your knuckles all over the affected area.

4 Roll your knuckles over the left buttock, and down along the left thigh, for three minutes, coming back up to the lower back. Finish by placing the palm of your left hand on the sacrum again, and hold it there for three breaths, imagining that you are breathing toward your sacrum. Turn on your left side and repeat the steps using your right hand.

41

in your
bathroom
soothing

find inner calm by combining
massage with warm water

1 Lie in the bath, and place the index, middle and ring fingers of both hands on your temples. If it is more comfortable, support your head on a pillow. Keep your fingers together, creating a flat surface. Close your eyes and breathe deeply and slowly three times, feeling the connection between your fingers and your temples.

2 (*opposite*) On the out-breath, press the pads of your fingers gradually into your temples, keeping your fingers together and flat. Hold, counting to three. On the in-breath, release the pressure, then start to press into your temples again with your next out-breath, and hold. Repeat three times.

3 Start making another "press-in" sequence, but this time don't release the pressure; instead make five slow, small, precise circles. To avoid stretching your skin, concentrate on moving the tissue underneath, rather than the skin itself.

4 Return to step 2, and make three "press-ins" each time, then three when you hold and make circles. Finish by placing both hands over your face, and breathing deeply.

43

1 *(right)* As you don't need to apply oil or cream for this invigorating massage, you can keep your socks on. Place your left foot on your right knee. Rub the foot between your palms, with your hands moving forward and backward in opposite directions, until your foot is warm.

2 Grasp the toes with your right hand, flexing and extending them rhythmically. Then work on each toe, starting from the big one and squeezing them several times between your thumb and index finger. Apply firm pressure, and make sure that you support the left foot with your left hand all the time you are working on the toes.

3 Work between the tendons on the top of the foot. Using the thumb of your right hand, press between each two toes, then run your finger from their base toward the ankle. Support your foot by holding the ankle with your left hand.

4 Come back to the sole of the left foot. With your fingers supporting your foot from the top, start walking the thumbs of both hands vigorously along the sole. Begin at the top of the sole and walk all the way down, toward the heel. Walk up and down for three minutes. Make sure that you keep the same rhythm all the time. Change over to the other foot, and then repeat all four steps again.

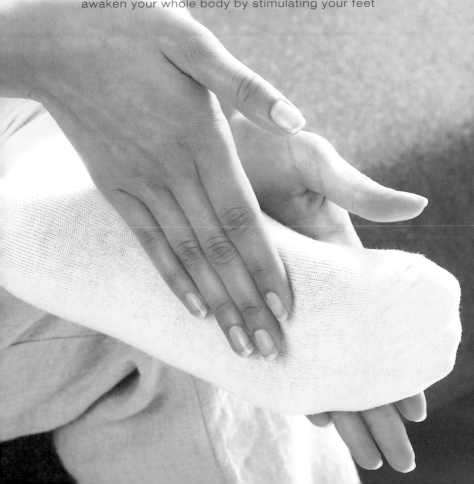

on your sofa
invigorating

awaken your whole body by stimulating your feet

at the park
refreshing

take time out in the open air to refresh your body

1 Sit on a bench or the grass, back supported, legs uncrossed, and hands resting on your lap. Hold your right wrist in your left hand. Rotate your right hand slowly from the wrist, keeping your arm still, five times in one direction and five in another. Drop your hand down and shake it vigorously several times. Repeat with your left hand.

2 Hold your right wrist in your left hand, and, while supporting it with your fingers, lightly press your thumb on the inner, soft part of the wrist, working from the edge of the palm toward the forearm. Hold each pressure for a count of two. Be careful to apply only gentle pressure, as there are lots of blood vessels in this area.

3 Squeeze your wrist in your left hand and hold, then move up your arm, squeeze and hold. Work along the forearm until you reach the elbow. Every time you squeeze another part of the forearm, breathe out.

4 Place your right arm along your right thigh, palm facing down. On your out-breath, press the fingers of your left hand into the top of your right wrist. Hold. On the in-breath, move your fingers up along the forearm slightly, press in, and hold while you breathe out. Work all along the forearm. Change arms and repeat steps 1–4.

47

1 Lie down on your back, in a comfortable position, with your arms at your sides and legs slightly apart. If you have a sore lower back, you can place a small pillow or rolled-up towel under your knees to decrease the pressure on the lower part of your spine.

2 (*right*) Place the ball under your neck. Make sure that you don't hold your neck up, but instead let it rest completely on the ball. Breathe deeply, allowing the ball to hold your neck. Try to increase the sensation of sinking your neck into the ball more deeply with each breath.

3 On the out-breath, start to roll your head over the ball, working from the middle to the right and back to the middle. Take in a breath, and when you start to breathe out, roll your head to the left side and back to the middle. Repeat several times, making each movement slow.

4 Change the rhythm, rolling all the way over from left to right on the out-breath, and from right to the left on the in-breath. Work three times in each direction. Don't increase the speed, as you need to be aware of every movement in your neck: it should feel like the space between each vertebra is loosening up. Come back to the neutral position, and breathe deeply, letting your neck rest on the ball.

at the beach
balancing

ease your neck with a massage that
uses a soft, air-filled ball

1 Before you start this massage, try to switch off your mind by closing your eyes and breathing deeply several times. Make sure that your shoulders stay relaxed. Slowly open your eyes and, on your out-breath, press your right thumb firmly but gradually into your left palm. Use the other fingers of your right hand to support the left hand.

2 (*right*) Make three firm, slow circles with your thumb, in both directions, pressing deeply into your palm. Move to any other point, and make another three circles. Make sure that the other fingers of your right hand support the left hand, and that you breathe regularly. Work over the whole palm, then change hands and repeat.

3 Squeeze the index finger of your left hand from its base, between the knuckles of the index and middle finger of your right hand. Pull and twist, right up to your fingertips. Work in the same way on each finger, and then change hands.

4 Lift both your shoulders as close to your ears as possible, and then drop them down. Repeat this movement three times. Return to a neutral position, shoulders relaxed and hands by your sides. Finish by shaking your hands vigorously five times.

at your desk
soothing

release tension from your hands,
and relax your mind

in a hotel room
invigorating
restore your energy between flights and meetings

1 (*left*) Sit straight, your feet flat on the floor. Place a hand either side of your head, fingers spread, little fingers on the hairline at the centre of your forehead. Close your eyes, breathe deeply. On an out-breath, press your palms into your scalp, and slowly lift. Hold for three seconds, then release. Repeat three times.

2 Supporting the left side of your head with your left hand, press your right palm into the right side of your scalp. Moving all over the right side, make circles with your palm. Breathe slowly and regularly, and imagine tension slowly melting away.

3 Change hands, supporting your scalp with your right hand. Press your left palm into the scalp, making circles, as in step 2, over the left side of your scalp.

4 Use the palms of both hands to make circles, lifting and rotating the whole scalp for 30 seconds. Start very slowly, then gradually increase the speed of your circles. Open your eyes. Finish by breathing deeply three times.

53

1 (*right*) While sitting comfortably in your seat, head and shoulders relaxed, place both hands on the tops of your knees, as if you are embracing the knee with your hand. You should feel your kneecap in your palm. Close your eyes and breathe deeply three times.

2 On the next out-breath, make five firm, short circles in an anti-clockwise direction over your knees, using your palms. Stop. Breathe in, and on the next out-breath make another five circles, this time in a clockwise direction. The more vigorously and rhythmically you carry out these movements, the more you will boost your circulation.

3 Try to keep your legs still, but relaxed. Next, tap along the tops of your thighs with the edges of your palms, in an alternating rhythm, working from the knees toward the pelvis, and back to the knees again. Repeat three times.

4 Place both your hands on the tops of your knees again, and then repeat the massage sequences given in steps 1 and 2. Finish with several deep breaths, then hold your hands on your knees for 60 seconds. Open your eyes and slowly release your hands.

on a plane
boosting

help prevent blood-flow stagnating,
especially in your legs and feet

stress
busters

Massage away your stress! You can use massage to help you cope more

easily with physical and emotional problems, and speed up recovery.

A regular, short massage will help you to relax within a couple of

minutes, restoring the whole system.

1 (*right*) Sit in a comfortable postion and place the fingers of both hands along your hairline. Make sure that the little fingers touch each other. With an out-breath, press gently into the hairline and, maintaining pressure, make three circles outward in opposite directions.

2 Place the fingers of each hand along the middle line of your scalp. Make sure that the little fingers are touching the hairline. Breathing out, press gently into the scalp and, as you did on the hairline, make two circles outward in opposite directions with every out-breath.

3 Lift your fingers, and place them further along the middle line. Your little fingers should now be where the index fingers were in step 2. Breathing in, press gently into the scalp and, with an out-breath, make two circles as you did before, taking care to maintain pressure.

4 Move your fingers to the base of your scalp. After the bump at the base, you will feel a little groove. Using your index and middle fingers, press into this area on the out-breath and hold, counting to five. Release, and repeat again. Finish by resting your hands on top of your head, without applying any pressure, and breathing deeply twice.

scalp lifter
relaxing

a scalp massage will release tension
from your face and neck

lower back reliever
soothing

free up lower back muscles and joints, where stress shows first

1 Sit comfortably, legs slightly open. Place your palms each side of the sacrum (lowest part of the back), making sure that you don't press directly on the spine. Rub your palms up and down the sacrum vigorously for 30 seconds, to warm up the muscles. Stop, holding your palms on the sacrum, and breathe in and out three times. Repeat twice.

2 Place the fingers of both hands along both sides of the spine, without pressing directly on the spine. Breathe in, pressing gently into the muscles, and make circles on your out-breath, concentrating on each sore spot. Continue pressing and circling for one minute, breathing regularly.

60

3 To increase pressure, form a fist and roll your knuckles along your lower back, starting from the sacrum and working up along the spine as high as is comfortable for you.

4 Roll your knuckles down toward your sacrum again, and make slow, firm circles over each buttock. Using the same movement, move to your hip muscles and make five circles with your knuckles. Finish by placing both your palms on the sacrum, and breathing regularly three times.

body relaxer
releasing

use deep breathing to release
physical and emotional tension

1 Make sure that your clothing is loose, with no tightness at the waist. Stand or lie down, with both arms relaxed at your sides. Close your eyes and take a deep breath in through your nose, directing it toward your belly. Allow your abdominal muscles to relax. Feel the breath sinking into your body. Exhale through your mouth.

2 (*opposite*) Place whichever hand is most comfortable for you palm down, on your abdomen, with the other hand resting above it. This will help you to direct the breath right there. Continue breathing with closed eyes, and feel your abdomen rise rhythmically with your in-breath, then sink down with the out-breath.

3 Drop your arms back down to your sides and then take another in-breath through your nose. Breathe out naturally, pausing at the end of the out-breath for a second or two before taking another in-breath.

4 Pause for as long as is comfortable and safe for you, and repeat. In the beginning, the pause will probably be very short as you might worry that your body is not filling up with breath. Accept this feeling and allow yourself to explore the pause, relaxing more every time.

eye calmer
refreshing

restore your eyes fast, giving a sense of harmony and peace

1 Sit in a comfortable position, eyes closed, neck and shoulders relaxed. Alternatively, lie with a pillow under your head and another under your knees to improve blood-flow in your legs. Place the fingers of your hands over your eyes. Breathe deeply, and imagine that you are directing every out-breath to your arms, hands and eyes.

2 Remove your hands, and place each middle finger in each inner corner of your eyes. With an out-breath, press gently into each corner with the finger pads, and hold, counting to five. Release, and repeat. Press all over underneath the eyes, holding and counting to five, until you reach the outer corners of your eyes.

64

3 Using your index fingers and thumbs, squeeze the eyebrows above the inner corner of your eyes and hold for five, then release. Work along your eyebrows from the bridge of your nose until you reach your temples, squeezing the eyebrows, then holding, counting to five, and releasing. Repeat.

4 Tap gently under your eyes and over your eyelids, using the finger pads of both hands. This movement should be light and rhythmical. Continue for 30 seconds, then cup both palms over your eyes, breathing deeply three times. Slowly open your eyes.

65

1 (*right*) Place the index, middle and ring fingers of each hand on each side of your jaw. To be sure that you cover the muscle fully, clench your teeth. You should feel the muscle move under your fingers, which will indicate that you have found the correct position. Close your eyes.

2 Breathe in, and with your out-breath press into the muscle on its highest point, just under the cheek arch, close to the ear lobe. Make five slow circles, pressing with your middle and ring fingers. Breathing regularly, work down along the muscle until you reach the corner of the jaw. Continue making circles as you come back up to the cheek arch. Repeat the sequence three times, keeping your breathing regular.

3 Place your thumbs on the corners of your jaw, fingers resting on your head. Taking a deep breath, open your mouth slightly. As you breathe out, press your thumbs gradually into your jaw, and hold. Slowly release. Repeat three times, feeling the jaw relax more each time.

4 Move to the next point, working with your thumbs from the top of your jaw down to the corners as in step 2, but this time just press and hold for five seconds in each place. Finish by resting your fingers softly along your jaw muscles and breathing deeply three times.

jaw reliever
relaxing

even a short massage
can ease pain and relax your jaw

foot de-stresser
releasing

de-stress your body in minutes by stimulating points on your foot

1 Sit comfortably, and place your right foot on your left knee. Supporting the heel of your foot with your left hand, press into the arch of the foot, using your right thumb. In reflexology, the arch corresponds to the spine, which is the first place to be affected by stress. Make as many small, firm circles as you like all over the arch.

2 Now concentrate on the pad below your big toe, which corresponds to the stomach. Supporting the foot with your left hand, press into the pad with the thumb of your right hand, and make five deep, slow circles.

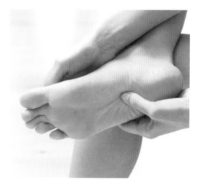

3 Slide your thumb down to the middle of your sole, where a small area corresponds to the kidneys and adrenal glands. Pressing in, make five small, deep circles, still supporting the foot with your left hand.

4 Repeat steps 1–3 in the large area between the middle of your sole and your heel, which relates to the intestines. As a rule, if you find a tender spot it shows that the organ related to that point is under stress. Focus on these areas, breathing deeply, and imagining that you are breathing away tension. Repeat on the other foot.

1   (*right*) Bend your neck forward slightly, and place the middle fingers of both hands in the grooves situated on both sides of your neck vertebrae, at the base of your skull. Don't apply pressure, just breathe deeply and feel the connection between your fingers and your neck.

2   With an out-breath, gradually apply pressure into both grooves (on both sides of your neck vertebrae), using your middle fingers. While pressing, you should bring your neck upright simultaneously, as this will enable you to press into a deeper layer of the muscles.

3   Maintaining pressure, make five circles with your middle fingers, breathing slowly and regularly. Release the pressure gradually, move your fingers slightly apart, and then apply pressure again. Make another five slow, precise circles.

4   Move your fingers sideways along the base of your skull to a new point, with your fingers just underneath the skull bone, and press into the muscles. Make five slow, precise circles, breathing regularly. Gradually release and move your fingers to the next point. Aim to change position five times, until you reach the corner of the bone, just behind your ears. Each time, you should be able to increase the pressure as your neck muscles relax more. Finish by breathing deeply three times.

neck balancer
unwinding

restore your energy in the middle of the day

mood enhancers

People who feel happy and have a positive approach to life tend to be

healthier than those who are more negative. You will find that simple

self-massage can dramatically lift your mood, slowing down the ageing

process, and bringing joy and vitality into your life.

chest booster
uplifting

use this technique to lift your spirits after a disappointment

1 Sit with your neck and shoulders relaxed. Place your right palm on the left side of your chest, close to the shoulder. Make a long, gentle stroke across your chest; sweep off when you reach the right shoulder. Place your left palm on your right chest, and stroke across, sweeping off at the left shoulder. Repeat the whole sequence five times.

2 Place the fingers of both hands along your collarbone. Starting from the middle, make five firm, slow circles. Move to the next point along. Press your fingers in, and make another five circles. Move to another point and continue all along the collarbone until you reach the edge of your shoulder.

3 Make loose fists and rest them gently in the middle of your chest. Press in deeply with both thumbs. Massage between your ribs, using your knuckles to make circles and pressing in with your thumbs all the time. Work all over the chest, breathing regularly.

4 Rest your fists lightly on your chest, but don't press your thumbs in. With an out-breath, tap rhythmically over your chest. Start slowly, gradually increasing speed, while keeping pressure light. Stop to take in breath, and start again with each out-breath. Repeat three times. Finish by placing your hands flat on your chest; breathe deeply twice.

CHEST BOOSTER

foot reviver
boosting

a super-fast mood reviver, as feet connect to all your organs

1 Sit on a chair, with your right foot resting on your left knee. Alternatively, you can sit cross-legged on the floor if that is comfortable for you. If you can't get your foot on top of your left knee, rest it on the floor in front of your knee. Keep your back straight and relaxed.

2 Place the toes of your right foot between both palms, making a sandwich. Rub the toes, moving your palms forward and backward in a fast, rhythmical way. Continue for at least 30 seconds, or until you start to feel a warmth in the upper part of your foot.

3 (*left*) Move to the middle part of the foot. Squeeze the middle of the sole and the top of the foot gently between both palms, and start to rub vigorously. You can vary the speed, increasing and decreasing gradually. Continue for 30 seconds, or until you feel warmth spreading from the foot to the upper leg.

4 Support the ankle of the right foot with your right hand. Place your left palm along the sole of the right foot, and rub along the whole sole vigorously, from the heel up to the toes. Continue for at least 30 seconds. Change over to the other foot and repeat steps 1–4.

1 Sit or lie down. Lift your hands to your face, but make sure that you don't lift your shoulders – keep them relaxed all the time. Place the fingers of both hands on your forehead. Press gradually into the tissue, and make as many circles as you need to cover your forehead. It is important that you don't slide over the skin, stretching it unnecessarily, but rather move the tissue, which lies underneath.

2 (*right*) Continue making circles for 30 seconds, then move to the cheeks. Press your fingers against the cheekbones and make circles without stretching the skin. Continue for 30 seconds, then move to the jaw, pressing into the jawbone, before you start to make five circles.

3 Place both palms over your face, and, keeping them loose, make light, upward strokes, starting from the jaw line and sweeping off on the forehead. You can create an uplifting sensation very quickly if you keep to light, rhythmical strokes.

4 Using the pads of the fingers of both hands, tap all over your face gently, starting on the forehead, then working lightly around your eyes, and slightly more firmly on the cheeks and jaw. Start slowly, increasing the speed gradually. The movement should be like light rain drops.

78

face lifter
restoring

release tension from your
face to restore your spirits

abdominal soother
balancing

massage your abdomen to leave you calmer and more tranquil

1 For maximum relaxation, carry out this massage unclothed, using some massage oil. Lie down and place your hands on your abdomen, palms down. Breathe deeply. Feel your abdomen rising and sinking with your in- and out-breath. Try to be aware of your the effects on your mood – you should feel calmer and more relaxed.

2 Stroke your abdomen with one hand after another, working in a clockwise direction and maintaining the constant flow of the movement as you gently lift and replace the hands.

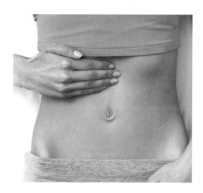

3 Use the fingers of your right hand to make small circles all around your abdomen, following its outline in a clockwise direction. These circles should connect with your breathing. If you want to, place one hand on the top of the other and increase the pressure to reach a deeper layer of muscle.

4 Press both palms flat across the lowest part of your abdomen, and stroke alternately upward, along your middle. While one hand is sweeping off below your chest, the other hand starts stroking upward from below your navel, maintaining a rhythmic, flowing movement. Finish by repeating step 1.

81

head booster
invigorating

whisk away your low mood with a stimulating massage

1 Sit, feet connected with the floor. Breathe deeply, feeling energy coming from your feet and travelling toward your hands. Place your hands on each side of your head, fingers pointing upward. On an out-breath press your hands slowly toward each other. Hold, count to three, and slowly release. Repeat three times.

2 Using relaxed, curled fingers, make circles all over your scalp. Keep your fingers firmly in place so that you move the skin against the bone. You shouldn't be able to hear any sound of the hair rubbing against the scalp. Make every circular movement dynamic and invigorating.

3 Support your head with your left hand and, using the flat fingers of your right hand, rub lightly and vigorously all over the surface of your scalp. Rub backward and forward, up and across, making sure that you cover the whole of your head.

4 (*opposite*) Continue rubbing backward and forward, but this time use the palms of both hands at the same time, and rub all over the scalp, starting from the hairline and finishing on the base of the scalp. Maintain the speed and dynamism of the movement throughout.

83

neck warmer unwinding

free up communication by easing stiffness in your neck

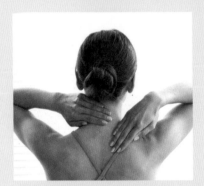

1 Stand or sit, and relax your shoulders. Make alternate strokes down your neck, starting from the back of your head and sweeping off on the back of the shoulders. When one hand reaches the shoulder, the other should start the stroke from the back of the head. Keep the flow going, and you will start to feel the muscles warming up.

2 Place your left hand over the left side of the neck for support, and bend the head slightly. Place the edge of your right palm against the base of your skull, and rub lightly but vigorously up and down, all over the base of the scalp, starting from the middle and going out toward the ear, and maintaining a constant rhythm throughout.

3 Supporting the head with the left hand, spread the thumb and fingers of the right hand around the neck. Squeeze the neck between your thumb and fingers, starting from the base of the scalp and going down to the base of the neck. Repeat three times.

4 When you reach the base of the neck, grasp the flesh there between thumb and fingers and pull it back. Slide to the middle of the neck, grasp flesh again and pull it back. Then slide to the base of the skull, grasp and pull flesh again. Repeat steps 3 and 4, changing hands and using the right hand to support and the left one to massage.

1 *(right)* Sit comfortably, with your neck relaxed and your head slightly bent. Place the middle fingers of both hands under your cheekbones on each side of the nose. There are shiatsu points located here, one on either side of the nose, which relate to the sinuses.

2 On the out-breath, gradually start to apply pressure. You can press quite strongly as long as you find it comfortable. Hold, counting to five, while you breathe in. On an out-breath, slowly release the pressure. Repeat the whole sequence three times. Move your fingers to another spot along the cheekbone, toward the ear, and apply pressure again. Repeat the sequence in the next spot along, until you reach your ear.

3 Next, unless you're pregnant, find the shiatsu headache spot, between your thumb and index finger. Locate the point by pressing around until you get a distinctive feeling. Press your right-hand thumb into your left palm several times, holding, and counting to five.

4 Change hands, and repeat step 3, pressing the left-hand thumb into the right palm. Then repeat the nasal and the hand acupressure sequences (steps 1–2 and step 3) one more time. Finish by cupping the palms of both hands over your face and breathing deeply three times.

sinus
clearer
restoring

open up your sinuses,
reducing headaches

energy
boosters

Massage is the best stimulant ever! When you feel that your energy

levels are dropping, instead of reaching for the coffee or the sugary

snacks, just spend five minutes on one of these techniques. You will

speed up your circulation, tone your muscles, and revitalize your

energy immediately, so you can face the world again.

1 Sit up straight and embrace yourself by placing your palms, with your fingers widely spread, as high up as possible on both outsides of your arms. Press your palms and fingers firmly into the upper arm muscles. Breathe out, squeezing and slowly massaging the muscles using your fingers and the middle edges of your palms.

2 Slide your hands down your arms, and embrace yourself just above the elbows. On the out-breath, squeeze the muscles and slowly massage them. Use your fingers for massaging the outer part of the muscles, and your thumbs for massaging the inner part. Repeat steps 1 and 2 three times, massaging your arms in both positions each time.

3 Embrace yourself, reaching as far as you can. On the out-breath, slowly stretch out your shoulderblades without lifting them. At the same time, bend your head slowly, creating stretch along the spine and between the shoulderblades. Hold for a count of five, and slowly release.

4 (*right*) Place your arms behind your back, holding the right wrist with the left hand. Breathing out, slowly stretch your shoulders as far back as is comfortable, opening the chest and collarbones. Try to feel the shoulderblades touching each other. Hold for a count of five; release.

shoulder stretcher

reinvigorating

massage and stretches release tension from your upper back

face booster
uplifting

acupressure restores energy flow all over your body

1 Lie down, with one small pillow under your knees and a second under your neck. Rest for a while, eyes closed, and arms by your sides. Breathe deeply. With every breath try to relax your body and mind more deeply.

2 Place your right-hand middle finger just below your hairline, in the middle of your forehead. With an out-breath, press in, using the pad of your finger. On the next out-breath make five slow, small circles in one direction. Stop, take a breath, and as you breathe out make five circles in the opposite direction. Move down and repeat.

3 The next point is slightly below the middle of your forehead. Press in while you take a breath and, on the out-breath, make five circles in one direction. Breathe in and press, then on the out-breath make five circles in the other direction. Slide down to the next point, between the eyebrows, press in gradually and repeat the sequence.

4 You will find the last two points on the nose. Starting in the middle, where there is a little groove, repeat the slow breathing, pressing and circling sequence. Then apply the sequence to the final point, on the tip of your nose. Don't worry if you can't find the point at first. With practice, your fingers will locate its energy-flow easily.

1 Sit straight, or stand. Place both hands on either side of the neck, where it connects to the shoulders. Don't apply any pressure yet. Just hold your hands, close your eyes, and breathe deeply three times, feeling the connection between your hands and the base of your neck.

2 (*right*) Bend your head back, and squeeze the muscles on each side of the base of the neck with your fingers and thumbs. The amount of muscle you are able to grasp will depend on how tense your neck and shoulders are. If you can't squeeze any portion of the muscles, just press your palms against the muscles as firmly as you can.

3 Slowly roll your head forward on an out-breath, squeezing the muscles all the time. You'll feel a nice stretch between the shoulder tops and the base of your neck. Bend your head forward as far as you can, squeezing the muscles. Hold, counting to ten and breathing deeply.

4 Slowly, return your head to the upright position. Next, repeat steps 2 and 3 twice, returning your head to the upright position between each sequence. Finally, finish the massage by placing both your palms flat, on either side of your neck, and breathing deeply.

neck reviver

restoring

a great break when you feel that
your energy level is dropping

thigh booster
reviving

improve your blood and energy flow after sitting for a long time

1 Sit straight, with your legs slightly open. Place the palms of both hands on the top of your right thigh and warm up the muscles by making long, vigorous strokes along the thigh, up and down. Keep the strokes rhythmical.

2 Form fists with both hands and place them on top of the right thigh. Press thumbs into the top of the thigh for better support, and make circles using your knuckles. Work all over the top of the thigh, then on the inner and outer part as well. Keep the movement dynamic, and breathe deeply.

96

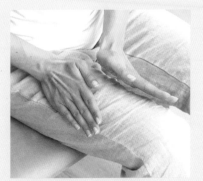

3 Place your flat palms on the top of the thigh and lift your fingertips so only the middle of the edges of the palms are touching your leg. Tap all over the thigh, using the edges of both palms, and working up and down, covering the top, inner and outer parts of the thigh. Try altering the speed and pressure.

4 Place the middle edge of your right palm just above your right knee and massage firmly, using circular pressure. Place your left hand on the inner part of the right knee for support. Carry this out this much more slowly than previous steps, making sure that your breathing is regular and deep. Repeat on your left thigh.

97

ear reviver
stimulating

working on reflex points in your
ears energizes your whole body

1 This is one of the easiest massages; you can practise it while you are sitting, standing, or lying down. If you are wearing earrings, remove them before you start. Close your eyes. Make sure that you breathe regularly during the massage.

2 Squeeze your ears between your thumbs and first two fingers. Starting at the lobe base, press, squeeze and knead until your scalp feels warm. Walk your fingers up around the outside to the top of your ear, massaging firmly as you go. Return to the lobe, squeezing between thumb and two fingers for a count of five.

3 (*left*) Twiddle your ears, using your thumbs and index fingers, and in the same direction and over the same area as in step 2. Do this three times. Your ears should feel hot now, and you might even experience a tingling sensation over your ears and face – a sign of free energy-flow.

4 Squeezing the tops of your ears between your thumbs and index fingers, pull up on your ears gently and rhythmically five times. Finish by squeezing the lobe between your thumbs and index fingers and pulling down gently and rhythmically five times. Open your eyes.

99

1 Stand with your legs slightly open. Make sure that your knees are not locked, as this would disturb the energy flow. Close your eyes. Place your hands, palms down, on both sides of your lower back. Hold gently, and send the breath toward your back. With every breath, feel the tension releasing slowly. Keep your eyes closed.

2 (*right*) Form tight fists with both hands, and start to tap vigorously, but not very fast, along both sides of your lower back between the vertebrae, using both fists at the same time. Set a consistent rhythm, and make sure that you don't tap over your spine.

3 Continue tapping, and move out from the middle of your lower back toward the hips. Spend extra time on both buttocks, tapping firmly and vigorously. Make sure that the buttock muscles are relaxed and your wrists are loose. Breathe regularly.

4 Return to the middle of the lower back, tapping all the time. Move up toward the shoulders, tapping both sides of the back, either side of the spine, as high as is comfortable for you. Work up and down your back three times, and then repeat the sequence, starting at step 2, twice.

back
releaser
invigorating

unlock the reservoir of energy
locked in your lower back

body energizer
boosting

use one technique to supply your whole body with fresh energy

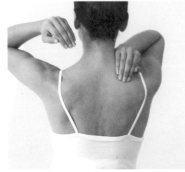

1 Stand with your arms relaxed and eyes closed, and breathe deeply several times. Open your eyes, and, starting from the shoulder and moving down to the hand, cup your left arm rhymically with the palm of your right hand. Move to a steady rhythm, and match your breathing to this. Repeat three times, change arm, and start again.

2 Using your right palm, cup vigorously along your left shoulder as far back as you can reach, for 15 seconds. Do the same on the other shoulder, using your left palm. Make sure that you maintain the rhythm, and that your wrist stays loose. It is important that you use cupping only on the fleshy areas, avoiding bony parts.

3 Move down to either side of your waist, and start cupping, first along your waist, then down along the hips, and up again toward the waist. Make sure that you stay on the sides of your body, avoiding the front, which is the site of all your organs.

4 Using both palms, cupping alternately, work on your legs, one at a time, covering the top, both sides, and the back of the thigh. Work vigorously for at least 15 seconds. Move to the lower leg. Concentrate on the back of the calf as the front is mostly bone. Cup in a steady rhythm for at least 15 seconds. Repeat on the other leg.

103

practising together

Massage is such a great way to show affection, respect and love. Don't wait for a long holiday to reward each other with healing touch. Practise these techniques as often as possible, bearing in mind that giving a massage can be as beneficial as receiving one.

1 (*right*) Stand in front of each other, knees slightly bent, and arms at your sides. Close your eyes and breathe deeply. Be aware of your partner's presence. Slowly reach for their hands without opening your eyes. Hold them for a moment, then while your partner keeps their hands still, start to explore the hands' shape and texture, using your fingers and thumbs. Imagine you have never touched them before.

2 Move very slowly and carefully, as if you are touching a precious, fragile object. Take as much time as you need. This will help you to maintain a light touch, which will give much more sensation than firm pressure. Now it is your partner's turn to try steps 1 and 2 on you.

3 It is your turn. Place both palms gently over your partner's face, without opening your eyes. Starting from the forehead, explore their face with your fingers. Look for signs of tension. Move over eyes and cheeks, then down to jaw and ears. Try to guess what this face wants "to tell you".

4 Allow your partner to discover your face while you are just present, open to receiving their touch. Be aware of sensations in your body. What kind of feelings surface? Finish by looking into each other's eyes, holding hands, and breathing together three times.

getting
connected
exploring

re-discover each other simply through touch

letting go
reviving

give your partner a shoulder massage when they arrive home

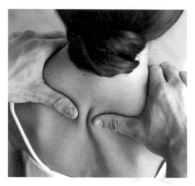

1 Ask your partner to sit in a chair, feet flat on floor, hands in their lap. Stand behind them, and place your left palm on their left shoulder and your right one on their right shoulder. Tell your partner to close their eyes and breathe deeply three times. Breathe deeply too, feeling the connection between your hands and their shoulders.

2 Squeeze the shoulder muscles between your fingers and thumbs, using as much of your hands as possible in order to avoid pinching your partner's skin. Lift and roll the muscles alternately, one side at a time, between your fingers and thumb.

108

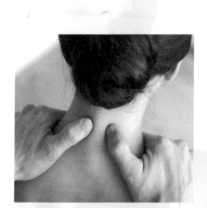

3 Place your thumbs either side of your partner's spine at the base of the neck, in the grooves between the vertebrae. Slowly press into these points simultaneously, and release. Move your thumbs down to the next space. Press again. Release slowly. Move down again, and repeat. Work along the spine, never pressing on it directly.

4 Standing to your partner's right side, reach across their chest to their left shoulder, placing one arm in front and the other behind. Interlock your fingers around their shoulder and squeeze the muscle between your palms. Hold for a count of five; release. Repeat, pressing into the middle of the shoulder. Repeat step 4 on the other shoulder.

109

1 While your partner is sitting down in a chair or on the floor, stand or kneel directly behind them and place both your hands on their shoulders. Ask them to breathe deeply as this will calm them down and help to release the tension that is stored in their back muscles.

2 Move to your left, and press your right palm edge into the muscles along the right side of your partner's lower back. As you press in, push the muscles away. Work over the lower back without pressing directly on the spine. Change sides, working in the same way on the left side.

3 Stand behind your partner again and, working where the tailbone is situated, using both thumbs, press into the muscles either side of the spine. Press into the muscles on your partner's out-breath, and release the pressure when they  are breathing in. Alternatively you can hold the pressure each time, counting to five, while your partner breathes deeply and regularly.

4 (right) With your left hand supporting your partner's back, apply circular pressure with the palm of your right hand on the lower part of the back. Strokes can be firm and vigorous, warming up the muscles and improving the blood circulation. Avoid putting pressure directly on the spine. Finish by placing both hands on your partner's shoulders again.

back relaxer
de-stressing

release your partner's tense muscles,
bringing harmony and calm

working together
restoring
at the end of the day, restore the bond between you both

1 (*left*) Sit on the floor, back to back, spines touching, legs comfortably crossed, and hands palms down on your knees. If you find the floor uncomfortable, you can sit on two small stools. If this is your choice, make sure that you sit with your feet flat on the floor, shoulders relaxed, and hands on your knees. Close your eyes.

2 Adjust your position against your partner's back, sitting straight so that you don't feel that you are leaning into each other too much. Without talking, start to breathe deeply, feeling your partner's presence.

3 Concentrate on your own breathing, directing your breath toward your abdomen. Be aware of all the thoughts passing through your mind and let them go. Observe the movement of the muscles in your back and belly while you are breathing. Stay in close connection with your partner's spine.

4 When you feel connected with your own body rhythm, tune in to your partner's breathing. Try to feel the movement of their back muscles, and follow the rhythm of your partner's breath. Feel their presence through their breath, and the gentle movement of their spine.

113

sleep enhancer relaxing

wish someone good night with a short face massage

1 Sit your partner on a chair and stand behind them, placing your hands gently on their head. Make sure that you don't apply any pressure with your hands, just hold. Ask your partner to breathe deeply three times. Now place both hands over their face, and make five gentle, light strokes from the middle of the face to either side.

2 Place the fingers of both hands flat on your partner's temples. Press in, and make five circles upward. It is important that you maintain pressure while you make circles, to avoid stretching the skin. You should make your circles very slow, concentrating on the layer of muscle under the skin.

114

3 Change position, moving your hands to your partner's jaw. Press into the muscles behind their teeth with your flat fingers, and make five small, firm circles. The jaw muscle is one of the body's strongest, so don't be afraid to apply firm pressure.

4 Using the fingers of both hands, stroke one hand after the other up the forehead, into the hairline. Stroke rhythmically, making sure that your hands are relaxed. Repeat five times: the repetitive movement is what makes the stroke so relaxing. Place your hands gently on your partner's head, and breathe together three times.

115

1

(*right*) Sit comfortably, facing each other. Take your partner's right hand and hold it in both your hands, while your partner breathes deeply. Place your hands either side of your partner's right lower arm. Squeeze and release the muscles using your hands alternately, working down to the wrist and then up again toward the elbow. Repeat three times.

2

Hold your partner's right hand between the fingers and thumbs of both your hands, sliding your thumbs over and gradually stretching out the top of their right hand with the edges of your thumbs. Repeat this three times, holding each hand stretch for three seconds.

3

Turn your partner's hand so that the palm is facing up. Place your left little finger between your partner's thumb and index finger, and your right little finger between the little and ring finger of your partner's hand. The rest of your fingers should be underneath your partner's hand.

4

At the same time, press down with your thumbs and up with your fingers, so that the palm stretches out slightly. Repeat three times, trying each time to achieve a deeper stretch in your partner's palm. Then use the thumbs to massage the palm, making five small, firm circles. Repeat steps 1–4 on your partner's left arm and hand.

116

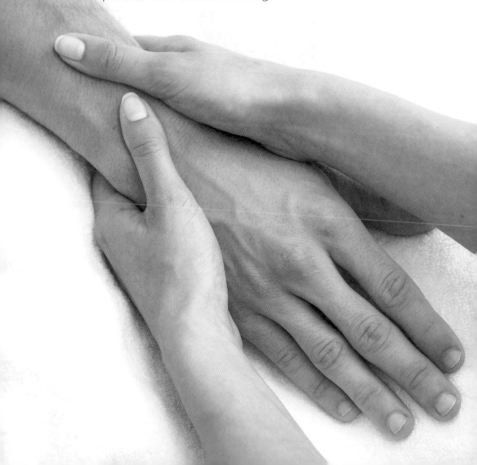

touching hands
soothing

show love and respect to your
partner with a hand massage

caring for feet
pampering

friends will be grateful for a relaxing, soothing foot massage

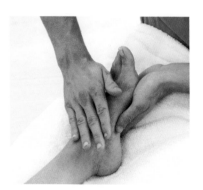
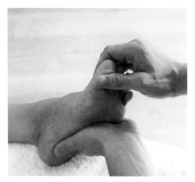

1 Hold your partner's left foot on your lap while you both sit comfortably, facing each other. Support the sole of your partner's foot with your left hand, and make long, rhythmical strokes over the top of their foot with the palm of your right hand. Stroke your hand rhythmically from their toes toward their ankle, warming up the foot.

2 Still supporting the foot with your left hand, squeeze your partner's big toe between the fingers and thumb of your right hand, and make five firm circles. Move to the second toe and repeat the sequence. Work on the other three toes one by one.

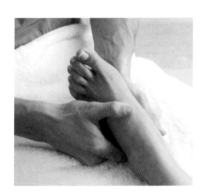

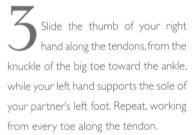

3 Slide the thumb of your right hand along the tendons, from the knuckle of the big toe toward the ankle, while your left hand supports the sole of your partner's left foot. Repeat, working from every toe along the tendon.

4 Form a fist with your left hand and slide it very slowly along the sole of your partner's foot, from the base of their toes to the heel. Hold the top of your partner's foot with your right hand, so that you can press against the top of their foot while you slide over the sole with your left fist. Change foot, and then repeat steps 1–4.

balancing
touch
caring

head massage is especially beneficial,
so offer a caring touch

1 *(left)* Ask your partner to lie down, head on the bed's edge. Sit on a chair, behind their head. Place both palms under their head, so they feel supported. Ask them to breathe deeply, and on an out-breath press your fingers under their scalp bone, where the neck connects. Hold, and slowly release. Repeat three times.

2 With your partner's head resting in your hands, lift it slightly, and drop it into your hands without any resistance. You should be able to feel its heaviness. Hold, counting to five. Lift a little more, then hold, counting to five, and lift even more, holding and counting to five. Slowly, gradually, lower the head back.

3 Slide your palms gently out from underneath your partner's head, place them on either side of their head and apply very light pressure. This can be very relaxing if you do it for at least 30 seconds.

4 Spread your fingers, and massage your partner's scalp with your finger pads. Press into the tissue first, then make at least ten slow, small circles. Ensure that you are moving the tissue underneath, rather than just rubbing the skin. Finish by holding your palms on either side of your partner's head for ten seconds.

121

tension reliever
releasing

offer to release tension in your partner's neck and shoulders

1 Ask your partner to sit comfortably, with their feet flat on the floor. Standing on their left, place your left hand on their forehead and stroke their neck with your right palm. Using long movements, start from the base of the neck and work down toward their shoulders. Your partner should feel a warmth over the neck area.

2 Supporting your partner's head with your left hand, hold their neck between your right-hand thumb and fingers. Make five circles with your thumb and fingers, moving from the base of the neck to the base of the scalp, back down and up again. Maintain a rhythm and keep the movement slow and gentle, as the neck can be sensitive.

3 When you reach the base of the scalp, continue making small circles with your thumb and the rest of your fingers on either side of your partner's head. Work out along the base of the scalp toward the ears in slow motion, until you reach the corner of the scalp bone, behind the ears.

4 When you reach the corner of the bone, come back to the middle point and start again, working in circles toward the ears. Repeat three times. Finish by covering the whole area of your partner's neck with the palm of your right hand. Hold for 30 seconds.

123

everyday sequences

If you are looking for a massage sequence when you have a little more time, use these menus to select the best one for you – soothing or invigorating, relaxing or energizing. You can try these massages in any suitable location.

half-hour unwinder

32 take a moment
66 jaw reliever
70 neck balancer
62 body relaxer
60 lower back reliever

half-hour calmer

64 eye calmer
30 lazy weekend
28 evening de-stress
42 in your bathroom
40 in your bedroom

half-hour uplifter

102 body energizer
74 chest booster
36 at a conference
82 head booster
44 on a sofa

one hour de-stress

62 body relaxer

64 eye calmer

78 face lifter

58 scalp lifter

66 jaw reliever

84 neck warmer

50 at your desk

68 foot de-stresser

40 in your bedroom

one hour reviver

102 body energizer

22 morning wake-up

100 back releaser

96 thigh booster

26 lunchtine lift

52 in a hotel room

92 face booster

86 sinus clearer

54 before a meeting

46 at a park

76 neck reviver

one hour energy booster

102 body energizer

92 face booster

52 in a hotel room

98 ear reviver

94 neck reviver

26 lunchtime energizer

90 shoulder stretcher

100 back releaser

96 thigh booster

44 on a sofa

46 at the park

index

abdominal soother 80–1

baby massage 8
back
  lower back massage 40–1
  lower back reliever 60–1,
   124
  relaxer 110–11
  releaser 100–1, 125
balancing massage
  abdominal soother 80–1
  at the beach 48–9
  before a meeting 34–5, 125
balancing touch 120–1
bathroom, in your 42–3, 124
beach, at the 48–9
bedroom, in your 40–1, 124,
  125
body energizer 102–3, 124,
  125
body relaxer 62–3, 124, 125
boosting massage
  body energizer 102–3, 124,
   125
  foot reviver 76–7
  on a plane 54–5

breathing 15, 16, 19
  body relaxer 62–3, 124,
   125

calming massage, half-hour
  calmer 124
caring for feet 118–19
caring massage, balancing
  touch 120–1
chest booster 74–5, 124
conference, at a 36–7, 124
connecting massage, shower
  time 24–5
contra-indications for massage
  13–14
couples 10

desk, at your 50–1, 125
de-stressing massage
  back relaxer 110–11
  in your bedroom 40–1, 124,
   125
  one hour de-stress 125

"each other" massage
  techniques 10–11

ear reviver 98–9, 125
energizing massage, lunchtime
  lift 26–7, 125
energy boosters 88–103
  back releaser 100–1, 125
  body energizer 102–3, 124,
   125
  ear reviver 98–9, 125
  face booster 92–3, 125
  neck reviver 94–5, 125
  shoulder stretcher 90–1, 125
  thigh booster 96–7, 125
evening de-stress 28–9, 124
exploring massage, getting
  connected 106–7
eye calmer 64–5, 124, 125

face massage
  face booster 92–3, 125
  face lifter 78–9, 125
  in your bathroom 42–3, 124
  sleep enhancer 114–15
focusing massage, take a
  moment 32–3, 124
foot massage
  caring for feet 118–19

evening de-stress 28–9, 124
foot de-stresser 68–9, 125
on your sofa 44–5, 124, 125
foot reviver 76–7

getting connected 106–7

half-hour sequences 124
hand massage
    at the park 46–7, 125
    at your desk 50–1, 125
    lazy weekend 30–1, 124
    touching hands 116–17
head massage
    balancing touch 120–1
    head booster 82–3, 124
    scalp lifter 58–9, 125
healing and massage 6–8
hotel room, in a 54–5, 125

invigorating massage
    back releaser 100–1, 125
    head booster 82–3, 124
    in a hotel room 54–5, 125
    morning wake up 22–3, 125
    on your sofa 44–5, 124, 125

jaw reliever 66–7, 124, 125

lazy weekend 30–1, 124
leg massage, on a plane 54–5
letting go 108–9
lower back reliever 60–1, 124
lunchtime lift 26–7, 125

meeting, before a 34–5, 125
mood enhancers 72–87
    abdominal soother 80–1
    chest booster 74–5, 124
    face lifter 67–9, 125
    foot reviver 76–7
    head booster 82–3, 124
    neck warmer 84–5, 125
    sinus clearer 86–7, 125
morning wake-up 22–3, 125

neck massage
    at the beach 48–9
    neck balancer 70–1, 124
    neck reviver 94–5, 125
    neck warmer 84–5, 125
    tension reliever 122–3

one hour sequences 125

pain 16
pampering massage
    caring for feet 118–19
    lazy weekend 30–1, 124
park, at the 46–7, 125
plane, on a 54–5
pregnancy 13

refreshing massage
    at a conference 36–7, 124
    at the park 46–7, 125
    eye calmer 64–5, 124, 125
reinvigorating massage,
    shoulder stretcher 90–1, 125
relaxing massage
    jaw reliever 66–7, 124, 125
    scalp lifter 58–9, 125
    sleep enhancer 114–15
releasing massage
    body relaxer 62–3, 124, 125
    foot de-stresser 68–9, 125
    tension reliever 122–3
restoring massage
    face lifter 78–9, 125

neck reviver 94–5, 125

sinus clearer 86–7, 125

working together 112–13

reviving massage

   letting go 108–9

   thigh booster 96–7, 125

rhythm 16–19

scalp lifter 58–9, 125

senior massage 8–10

shoulder massage 36–7

   giving to a partner 108–9

   tension reliever 122–3

shoulder stretcher 90–1, 125

shower time 24–5

silence 15–16

sinus clearer 86–7, 125

sleep enhancer 114–15

sleep patterns, evening

  de-stress 28–9, 124

sofa, on your 44–5, 124, 125

soothing massage

   at your desk 50–1, 125

   evening de-stress 28–9, 124

   lower back reliever 60–1,
    124

   in your bathroom 42–3, 124

speed of massage 16–19

stimulating massage, ear reviver

  98–9, 125

stress busters 56–71

   body relaxer 62–3, 124, 125

   eye calmer 64–5, 124, 125

   foot de-stresser 68–9, 125

   jaw reliever 66–7, 124, 125

   lower back reliever 60–1

neck balancer 70–1, 124

scalp lifter 58–9, 125

take a moment 32–3, 124

teenagers 10

tension reliever 122–3

thigh booster 96–7, 125

touching hands 116–17

unwinding massage

   half-hour unwinder 124

   neck warmer 84–5, 125

uplifting massage

   chest booster 74–5, 124

   face booster 92–3, 125

   half-hour uplifter 124

working together 112–13

acknowledgments

author's acknowledgments

I would like to thank Duncan Baird for giving me such a fantastic opportunity to share my thoughts and experience on touch with others, Grace Cheetham for inspiration, enthusiasm and real support, Judith More for guiding me through the complexity of the English language and for such wonderful editing, Manisha Patel for making the book look so beautiful, and my son Igor and my husband Jean-Marc for their love and for believing in me.

publisher's acknowledgments

Duncan Baird Publishers would like to thank models Sarina Carruthers and Adam Mommsen, hair and make-up artist Tinks Reding, and photographer's assistant Adam Giles.